Short Stories of Ryunosuke Akutagawa

Level 1
(1000-word)

Translated and Retold by Michael Brase

IBC パブリッシング

※本書はラダーシリーズ『杜子春 (Toshishun)』、『鼻 (The Nose)』、『藪の中 (In the Woods)』を再構成したものです。

はじめに

　ラダーシリーズは、「はしご(ladder)」を使って一歩一歩上を目指すように、学習者の実力に合わせ、無理なくステップアップできるよう開発された英文リーダーのシリーズです。

　リーディング力をつけるためには、繰り返したくさん読むこと、いわゆる「多読」がもっとも効果的な学習法であると言われています。多読では、「1. 速く 2. 訳さず英語のまま 3. なるべく辞書を使わず」に読むことが大切です。スピードを計るなど、速く読むよう心がけましょう（たとえばTOEIC® テストの音声スピードはおよそ1分間に150語です）。そして1語ずつ訳すのではなく、英語を英語のまま理解するくせをつけるようにします。こうして読み続けるうちに語感がついてきて、だんだんと英語が理解できるようになるのです。まずは、ラダーシリーズの中からあなたのレベルに合った本を選び、少しずつ英文に慣れ親しんでください。たくさんの本を手にとるうちに、英文書がすらすら読めるようになってくるはずです。

《本シリーズの特徴》
- 中学校レベルから中級者レベルまで5段階に分かれています。自分に合ったレベルからスタートしてください。
- クラシックから現代文学、ノンフィクション、ビジネスと幅広いジャンルを扱っています。あなたの興味に合わせてタイトルを選べます。
- 巻末のワードリストで、いつでもどこでも単語の意味を確認できます。レベル1、2では、文中の全ての単語が、レベル3以上は中学校レベル外の単語が掲載されています。
- カバーにヘッドホーンマークのついているタイトルは、オーディオ・サポートがあります。ウェブから購入／ダウンロードし、リスニング教材としても併用できます。

《使用語彙について》
レベル1：中学校で学習する単語約1000語
レベル2：レベル1の単語＋使用頻度の高い単語約300語
レベル3：レベル1の単語＋使用頻度の高い単語約600語
レベル4：レベル1の単語＋使用頻度の高い単語約1000語
レベル5：語彙制限なし

Contents

Toshishun 1

The Nose 41

In the Woods 69

Word List 104

Toshishun

唐の都、きらびやかな洛陽の街に、杜子春という若者がいた。かつて金持ちだったが今はその日の宿さえない彼に、不思議な老人が声をかけ、莫大な財産をもたらした。しかしその三年後、杜子春は再び文無しになっていた。不思議な老人は再び彼に財をもたらし、金は再び浪費しつくされた。三度目に老人が現れたとき、杜子春は金で態度を変える人々に嫌気がさしており、仙人である老人に弟子入りを志願した。老人はそれを許し、二人は空を飛んで峨眉山へと向かう……。

読みはじめる前に

Toshishun に出てくる語です。あらかじめ確認しておきましょう。

Tang	唐（＝中国）
Luoyang	洛陽。今の中国河南省河南。
Toshishun	杜子春（人名）。中国の古典、『杜子春伝』に由来。
follower	弟子
wizard	仙人
Tekkanshi	鉄冠子（人名）。中国の仙人左慈の道号に由来。
Mt. Gabisan	峨眉山。中国四川省にある山の名。
In the mornings...	呂洞賓の作による詩。仙術を用いて中国全土を飛び回るさまを詩う。
Seiobo	西王母。中国二大仙境の西方、崑崙山に住むという中国神話の女神。
evil spirits	魔性
demon warrior	神将
Hades	地獄
devil	鬼
Road of the Dark Hole	闇穴道。この世と地獄とを結ぶ道。
Never Ending Place	森羅殿。閻魔大王の宮殿。
King of Hades	閻魔大王
Sword Mountain, Blood Lake, Fire Valley, and Ice Sea	剣の山、血の池、焔の谷、氷の海。いずれも地獄の名称。

1

It was the evening of a spring day.

A young man stood near the West Gate of the Tang capital of Luoyang, looking up at the sky. His name was Toshishun. He was once the son of a rich man, but now he was poor. All the money he had was just enough to keep him going from day to day.

At this point in history, Luoyang was the greatest city on the face of the earth. People and carts moved up and down the streets without end. There were fine hats, expensive earrings, and wonderful horses. It was almost as beautiful as a picture.

But all this meant nothing to Toshishun. He still stood near the wall of the West Gate. He still looked up at the sky, where he saw the moon, long and white.

Toshishun said to himself, "The sun is going down. I am hungry, and I have no place to stay tonight. If this is all life has for me, I may as well throw myself into the river and die."

Then suddenly—who knows from where—an old man with one bad eye appeared in front of Toshishun. Standing against the setting sun, he threw an enormous shadow on the gate. He looked down into Toshishun's face and said, "What are you thinking?"

Toshishun replied, "Me? Since I don't have any place to sleep tonight, I was wondering what I should do." The old man's question had caught Toshishun by surprise, and so he had given a straight answer without thinking.

"Is that so? That's too bad," The old man said. And then, after thinking for a second, he pointed at the setting sun and spoke again. "Let me tell you something good. Stand in the setting sun so that you throw a shadow on the ground. At the place where the shadow of your head falls, dig a hole in the dark of night. You will find enough gold there to fill a cart."

Toshishun was surprised and said, "Is that true?" But when he looked up, the old man had disappeared. Instead, he saw the moon, which had become whiter than before, and two or three bats flying low in the sky.

2

On that day Toshishun became the richest man in all of Luoyang. It had happened just as the old man had said. In the dark of night, he had dug a hole where the shadow of his head had fallen in the setting sun, and he had found enough gold to fill a cart.

Toshishun soon bought a house and began to live a life of luxury.

When the word spread that Toshishun was rich, a great change took place among his friends. When he was poor, most of his friends would not even say hello if they met him on the street. But now that he was rich, they visited him day and night.

With each coming day, the number of visitors increased, until finally every person who could be called important had visited Toshishun's home. A party was held every day of the week, and each party was more wonderful than any Luoyang had ever seen.

But no matter how rich you are, there will come a day when there is no more money to spend. A year passed, and then another, and Toshishun became poorer and poorer. It was then that another great change took place among his friends.

Now, even if they were passing in front of his house, they would not stop by to say hello.

In the spring of the third year, Toshishun had spent all of his money and was now without a cent, just as before. In all of Luoyang, there was not a single person who would give Toshishun a place to stay for the night. Even worse, no one would even give him a glass of water.

One day in the evening, Toshishun found himself back at the West Gate, looking up at the sky. Then, just as before, the old man with a bad eye suddenly appeared before him and said, "What are you thinking?"

When Toshishun saw the old man's

face, he looked down in shame and didn't speak for a while. But, since the old man was kind, and since he was using the same words as before, Toshishun decided to answer in the same way: "Since I don't have any place to sleep tonight, I was wondering what I should do."

The old man said, "Is that so? That's too bad. Let me tell you something good. Stand in the setting sun so that you throw a shadow on the ground. At the place where the shadow of your chest falls, dig a hole in the dark of night. You will find enough gold there to fill a cart."

And as soon as he finished speaking, the old man disappeared, just as he had before.

The next day Toshishun once again became the richest man in Luoyang. And once again he began to lead a life of luxury. Everything was just as it had been before.

And just as before, all the gold that he had found in the ground disappeared in just three years.

3

"What are you thinking?"

For the third time the old man with a bad eye appeared in front of Toshishun and asked the same question. Toshishun was, as always, standing by the West Gate, looking up at the moon in the sky.

"Me?" said Toshishun. "Since I don't have any place to sleep tonight, I was wondering what I should do."

"Is that so? That's too bad. Let me tell you something good. Stand in the setting sun so that you throw a shadow on the ground. At the place where the shadow of your stomach falls, dig a hole in the dark of night. You will find enough gold there to fill—"

When the old man got that far, Toshishun suddenly raised his hand and stopped him. "No, I no longer want money," he said.

"You no longer want money? Ah, so you have grown tired of luxury, I see." The old man looked hard into Toshishun's face as he spoke.

"Tired of luxury?" said Toshishun. "Oh, not me. What I have grown tired of is people."

Toshishun went on. "People don't have

feelings—not true feelings. When I am rich, they are kind to me, and smile at me. But when I am poor, they won't even look my way. So who would want to be rich again?"

When the old man heard this, he broke out into a smile. "I see. Well, for someone so young, you learn quickly. From now on then, you will be poor, and you will be happy being poor."

Toshishun didn't know what to say. But finally he looked up and said, "Being poor and being happy at the same time is impossible for me. That is why I want to become your follower. You are a wizard, aren't you? Only a wizard could make me the richest man in Luoyang in one night.

Please, make me your follower. Teach me the wonderful ways of wizards."

The old man said nothing for a while as he seemed to work out some difficult problem in his head. Then he smiled and said, "You are right. I am the wizard who lives on Mt. Gabisan. I am known as Tekkanshi. The first time I saw your face, I thought you were a man who could learn quickly. That's why I twice made you rich. If you really want to become a wizard, then I will make you one."

These words made Toshishun feel not just glad but happy. As soon as Tekkanshi had spoken his last word, Toshishun fell to the ground before him and thanked Tekkanshi for being so kind.

"Oh, there is no need to thank me," Tekkanshi said. "Even if I take you on as my follower, whether or not you become a wizard is up to you. But, in any case, you should first come with me to Mt. Gabisan. Look, someone has left their bamboo walking stick behind. We can make use of it."

Tekkanshi picked up the bamboo stick, and after saying some strange words, he and Toshishun got on the stick as if it were a horse. Then the most surprising thing happened. The stick quickly rose up into the sky, almost as if it were a dragon, and went flying off toward Mt. Gabisan.

Toshishun was very surprised by this, and was almost afraid to look down at the ground below. When he did look, he saw blue mountains standing out in the light of the setting sun. Luoyang and its West Gate were nowhere to be seen.

Before long, Tekkanshi began to sing a song:

In the mornings, I play in the north sea;
   in the evenings, I go south to Mt. Sogo.
I have a blue snake up my sleeve,
   and a wonderful feeling in my heart.
Three times I have been to Gakuyo
   Town,
   but no one knew me for who I was.
Now, while singing a song,
   I fly high over Dotei Lake.

4

The bamboo stick and the two men soon came to rest on an enormous rock at Mt. Gabisan, which looked down into a deep valley. It was so high up that one of the brightest stars looked as big as a tea bowl. All around was quiet, because no one ever came there. The only sound was the singing of a pine tree in the night wind.

Tekkanshi had Toshishun sit down on the rock and said to him, "I am going to see Seiobo, the Mother of Wizards. You stay here until I come back. While I am gone, evil spirits will appear and try to tempt you. Whatever happens, do not say a word. Speak one word, and you cannot become a wizard. Do you understand?"

"I understand," Toshishun answered. "No matter what, I will not speak. No matter what, I will not say a word."

"Yes, that's it," said the old man. "Now I am off to the Mother of Wizards." With that, Tekkanshi got on the bamboo stick and flew straight toward the dark mountains that stood out against the night sky.

Toshishun was left by himself on the rock. An hour passed, and the cold mountain air began to make its way through his light clothes.

Then, Toshishun heard a voice.

"Who is that sitting there?"

It was an angry voice. But Toshishun said nothing, just as he had been taught by the old man.

After a while, he heard the same voice again. "Answer now or prepare to die."

Still, Toshishun said not a word.

Suddenly a tiger leaped up onto the rock. Its eyes were bright and angry. It looked hard at Toshishun, and let out a terrible cry.

But that was not all. An enormous white snake appeared and came toward him. Its tongue danced in and out of its mouth, the way a fire flickers at the windows of a burning building.

But Toshishun continued to sit where he was, not moving even one finger.

It seemed that the tiger and the snake both wanted the same thing—to have Toshishun for dinner. They each waited for their chance, looking hard at each other. Then, suddenly, they both came toward him.

Toshishun wondered which would get him first—the tiger or the snake. But then, all at once, both of them disappeared into the air, as if they had never been there at all. All that was left was the singing of the pine tree.

Toshishun was happy that he had come through the experience alive. Yet he couldn't help wondering what would happen next.

Just then, a terrible wind came up, and a black cloud came down to the ground and spread all around Toshishun. Next, the cloud was cut in half by a bright light, and a sound like a thousand drums came from the sky.

But that was not the end of it. It began to rain so hard that Toshishun thought it would never stop. But he was not afraid. Even in the hard rain, he sat quietly and did not move.

There was the sound of the wind, the rain and the water, and the bright lights going across the sky. It seemed that Mt. Gabisan would never be the same again.

Finally, there was another loud sound in the sky, and a ball of fire fell straight down toward Toshishun's head.

Toshishun put his hands over his ears and threw himself down on the rock. When he finally opened his eyes, he saw the sky as it was before, without a single black cloud. And high over the mountains was that same star, as big as a bowl for drinking tea.

It seemed to Toshishun that everything that had happened—the tiger, the snake, the wind and rain—was all the work of evil spirits. It was not real. This thought made him happy, and he sat down on the rock again.

But Toshishun did not feel happy for

long. This time a terrible demon warrior that was nine meters tall appeared before him. It was dressed in gold armor and carried a spear that had three points.

With anger in his eyes, the demon warrior pointed the spear at Toshishun's heart and said, "You there. Who do you think you are? Mt. Gabisan has been my home since the beginning of time. Now I find you here. Tell me who you are or lose your life."

But Toshishun did just as the old man had told him to do—he kept his mouth closed.

"So you are not going to answer? I see," said the demon warrior. "If that is the way you wish it, my followers must cut you into pieces."

The demon warrior raised his spear above his head, and his followers rose up from the mountains and filled the sky. Any minute they would come down and begin the work of cutting Toshishun into pieces.

Seeing this, Toshishun wanted to cry out for help, but then he remembered Tekkanshi's words. When the demon warrior saw that Toshishun was not afraid, he became so angry that his eyes grew big in his head.

"If you are going to be that way, then there is only one thing for me to do." The demon warrior then raised his spear, and with one quick move, he killed Toshishun.

In the next second the demon warrior disappeared, leaving behind nothing but a terrible laugh. Even his followers had gone, as if they were just a dream.

The big star in the sky looked down on Mt. Gabisan, spreading its light over the rock. The pine tree sang in the wind. Toshishun was still on the rock, his dead eyes looking up toward the sky.

5

Toshishun's dead body was still on the rock, but his spirit had already begun its fall down to Hades. Between this world and the world of Hades, there is a road that all people must travel. It is called the Road of the Dark Hole. No light falls on this road, and the wind there blows cold as ice.

Toshishun's spirit was carried like a leaf on the cold wind, going this way and that, until it came to rest in front of a large building. On the building was a sign that read, "Never Ending Place."

In front of Never Ending Place was an enormous number of devils. As soon as the devils saw Toshishun, they came around him. They brought him before a creature dressed in black and gold clothes. Toshishun was sure that this was the King of Hades. Afraid of what would happen next, Toshishun fell to the ground before the King.

"Who are you and why have you come to Mt. Gabisan?" The voice of the King of Hades was enormous, like the sound of a thousand drums. Toshishun was getting ready to answer the question, but then he remembered his promise to Tekkanshi. So Toshishun simply looked down and said nothing.

The King of Hades looked hard at Toshishun. "Do you understand where you are? Answer quickly or you will be sorry you were ever born."

Still, Toshishun said not a word. Seeing this, the King of Hades spoke to the devils in a low voice. The devils quickly took hold of Toshishun and flew high into the sky above the Never Ending Place.

As we all know, in Hades there are places like Sword Mountain, Blood Lake, Fire Valley, and Ice Sea. They are all to be found in the dark, black sky above Never Ending Place. Toshishun was dropped into these places, one after another. His body became one enormous pain—his head, his face, his tongue, his chest, his skin.

Still, Toshishun said not a word.

The devils had done everything they could to make Toshishun speak. They could do no more. So once again they flew up into the sky, but this time they flew back to where the King of Hades was waiting. With one voice, the devils said, "This human will not speak, no matter how much pain we cause him."

The King of Hades made a terrible face and fell into thought. Then he seemed to have an idea. "This human's mother and father are here in Hades. Bring them before me."

As soon as the King of Hades had

spoken, one devil flew like the wind up into the dark night. But no sooner had the devil gone than it was back again, driving two poor creatures before it.

When Toshishun saw the two creatures, he was more shocked than surprised. They looked like horses, but their faces were the faces of his own mother and father.

"Now, I ask again. Who are you and why have you come to Mt. Gabisan? If you do not answer quickly, your mother and father will be sorry."

Still, Toshishun did not answer.

"Do you think nothing of your mother and father? You think only of yourself?" The voice of the King of Hades was enormous, like the sound of a thousand drums.

Then the King of Hades gave an order to the devils. "Strike them, devils. Make them feel pain—terrible, terrible pain."

In one voice, the devils shouted, "Haaa." They picked up their whips and struck the two horses. The whips sang as they cut through the air and fell on the bodies of the horses—here, there, everywhere.

The horses—that is, Toshishun's mother and father—turned their bodies this way and that to keep away from the whips. Their eyes filled with tears of blood. They cried out in voices that would break your heart.

The King of Hades ordered the devils to stop and turned to Toshishun. "Now, are you ready to speak?"

The two horses were on the ground before the King. Their pain was a pain no one should ever have to feel.

Closing his eyes, Toshishun tried his best to remember Tekkanshi's words. Then he heard a voice. The voice was so low, so quiet, that it was almost not a voice at all. "Don't worry yourself. No matter what happens to us, don't worry—as long as you are happy. No matter what the King says, don't speak. Not if you don't want to."

It was the voice of Toshishun's mother, a voice he remembered so well. Without thinking, he opened his eyes. One of the horses looked sadly toward him. Even now, even in such great pain, Toshishun's mother thought only of her son.

When he was rich, people liked Toshishun. When he was poor, they no longer wanted to talk to him. But his mother, she thought of him always, no matter what the time, no matter what the place. What a wonderful person she was! What a good and simple human being!

Toshishun forgot the words of Tekkanshi. He ran to his mother and put his arms around her. Tears fell from his eyes as he cried, "Mother!"

6

The moment he heard his own voice say "Mother," Toshishun found himself back under the West Gate of Luoyang. Everything was just as it had been before he went to Mt. Gabisan—the setting sun, the sky, the moon, the people and the carts.

"What did I tell you? Just because you become my follower doesn't mean you can become a wizard." The old man with one bad eye smiled as he spoke.

"Yes, you are right," Toshishun said.

"You are right, and I am glad that you are right."

With tears in his eyes, Toshishun took the old man by the hand. "Even if it means I cannot become a wizard, I could not stand by while my mother and father were being put through such pain."

"If you had just stood by and said nothing…" Tekkanshi said, looking hard at Toshishun. "If you had just stood by and said nothing, I would have killed you myself. So, you don't want to be a wizard anymore. And you no longer want to be rich. What do you want to be?"

"No matter what I am, I want to live a good and simple life." Toshishun's voice had something in it that had not been there before.

"Don't forget that thought—don't let it go," Tekkanshi said. "Well, we will not be seeing one another again." And with that, Tekkanshi turned and walked quickly away.

But then he stopped and looked back. "Ah, I just thought of something," he said, with a smile on his face. "I have a little house in the south, on Mt. Taizan. It is yours, along with the fields around it. The peach trees there are pretty at this time of year."

The Nose

僧侶の禅智内供(ぜんちないぐ)は鼻が長いので有名だった。気にしていないふりをしていたが、禅智はずっと自分の鼻を嫌い、気に病んでいた。あるとき、京都に出かけた若い僧が、長い鼻を小さくする方法を聞いてきたという。禅智はたいして気乗りしない風を装いながらも、それを試してもらうことにした。湯に鼻をつけ、若い僧にその鼻を踏んでもらう。この方法は成功し、禅智は短くなった鼻を鏡に映してほほえんだ。しかし、その数日後……。

読みはじめる前に

The Nose に出てくる語です。あらかじめ確認しておきましょう。

Priest Zenchi	禅智内供（ぜんちないぐ）。内供は内供奉僧の略称で、高徳の僧
Ike-no-o Town	池の尾。京都府宇治市池尾町
monk	僧
sneeze	くしゃみをする
sutra	経典。ここではとくに仏教の経典
common people	一般人、庶民
bath house	湯屋
finger	〜を指でいじる
snake gourd	カラスウリ（ウリ科の多年草）
Chorakuji Temple	長楽寺
itch	かゆい
itchy	かゆい
oily bumps	角栓、皮脂の固まり
tweezers	毛抜き
copy a sutra	写経する
read a sutra out loud	読経する
statue	像
Fugen Bodhisattva	普賢菩薩
waste	浪費する
turn out	〜と判明する

There was no one in Ike-no-o Town who didn't know about Priest Zenchi's nose. It was between fifteen and eighteen centimeters long and hung from above his upper lip down to his chin. It was the same size around from one end to the other. In fact, Priest Zenchi's nose looked very much like a sausage that was growing from the middle of his face.

Zenchi was now over fifty years old. Ever since he was a young monk, he had not liked his nose. But that was something that he did not want people to know. After all, he was a priest and should be thinking about more important matters. But more than that, he didn't want people to know that he was almost always thinking about his nose. Even when he talked with people, he was afraid that someone would bring up the subject of noses.

The Nose

Priest Zenchi did not like his nose for two reasons. One was simply because a long nose caused a lot of trouble. He could not, first of all, eat by himself. If he did eat by himself, his nose would fall right into his bowl of rice. So Zenchi would have someone sit across the table from him and hold up his nose with a piece of wood sixty centimeters long. This was not an easy thing to do, either for the person holding the piece of wood or for the Priest himself. Zenchi once had a boy monk hold the piece of wood, but when the boy sneezed and lost his hold on the wood, he dropped Zenchi's nose straight into the rice. The story about Priest Zenchi's nose falling into a bowl of rice soon spread all the way to Kyoto.

But the trouble it caused was not the most important reason for Priest Zenchi not liking his nose. The most important reason was that his nose was not part of the image that he had of himself. For example, people living in Ike-no-o Town said that Zenchi was lucky to be a priest. They thought that if he were not a priest and he wanted a wife, he would never be able to find one because of his long nose. Some people even said that Zenchi may have become a priest in the first place because of his nose. But Zenchi himself thought that the trouble his nose gave him was about the same, priest or no priest. The image that Zenchi had of himself was too strong to be changed by whether or not he could get a wife.

Zenchi tried many things to keep this image as perfect as it could be. First, he thought of how he might make his nose look shorter than it really was. When no one was around, he would look at his face in a mirror this way and that. He tried to find the best way of holding his head to make his nose look different. But he soon grew tired of that. Next, he tried resting his chin on his hand or putting his fingers along his jaw. He looked hard into the mirror to see if this made his nose look any smaller. But his nose never looked smaller, not even once. There were even times when he thought that his nose was getting longer, no matter how hard he tried. When this happened, Zenchi would put the mirror away, sigh to himself, and return to his desk to read a sutra.

Second, not only did Priest Zenchi worry a lot about his own nose, he thought a lot about other people's noses, too. The temple in Ike-no-o was visited by a good number of priests and common people. Many priests lived there, and there was a bath house that was used every day. Priest Zenchi looked with great care at each person who came to the temple. If he could find just one who had a nose like his, he would be very happy.

The Nose

In Zenchi's eyes, clothing, hats, and such things were not important. In fact, Priest Zenchi did not really look at people or their clothes; he looked only at their noses. While he found some noses that pointed down like his did, he didn't find any that were close to his in shape. After this had happened many times, Zenchi felt sad about himself and his interest in noses. When he talked to people, Zenchi would finger the end of his nose without thinking. Then, when he discovered what he was doing, his face would get red like a little boy's. Priest Zenchi was not happy about his great interest in his own nose.

Finally, Priest Zenchi turned to reading books to find a person with a nose like his own. If he could find just one person, that would make him feel a lot better. But no matter what he read, he couldn't find a nose like his. When he learned that a Chinese emperor had large ears, he thought how wonderful it would be if those ears had been a nose.

Along with trying to find a long nose among living people and in books, Priest Zenchi also tried to change the size of his own nose. In fact, he tried everything he could, such as drinking medicine made from the snake gourd. But no matter how hard he tried, his nose continued to hang down fifteen to eighteen centimeters, just as before.

The Nose

But then, one autumn, a young monk from the temple went to Kyoto to do some business for Priest Zenchi. While there, this monk met a doctor, who was the friend of a friend. The doctor had come to Japan from China many years ago and was now a priest at Chorakuji Temple. From this doctor, the monk learned how to make a long nose short.

As always, Priest Zenchi did not want people to know that he could not stop thinking about his nose, so he did not try what the doctor said right away. When he was eating, he would often say, in a friendly way, how much trouble he was causing the young monk who held the piece of wood for his nose. But Zenchi really wanted to try the doctor's way to make his nose shorter. In fact, he was waiting for the young monk to tell him to do so. The young monk himself knew what Zenchi really wanted. He did not look down on Zenchi for playing this little game. He could understand Zenchi's feelings very well. So the young monk, saying this and that, tried to get Zenchi to follow the doctor's new way to make his nose smaller. Zenchi had hoped the young monk would do this. And then, just as the young monk hoped, Zenchi agreed to give the new way a try.

The doctor's new way was very simple: Zenchi's nose was put into hot water for a while, and then it was taken out and

The Nose

stepped on again and again by the young monk.

Hot water was made every day in the temple bath house. It was so hot that it could burn your fingers. This water was brought to Priest Zenchi, but if he put his nose straight into the water, he might burn his face. So a piece of wood with a hole in the center was put over the hot water, and Zenchi put his nose through the hole. Strange to say, his nose did not feel hot.

After a while the young monk would say, "I believe it is ready."

Hearing this, Zenchi smiled to himself. From these words alone, a person in the next room would never know that they were really talking about his nose. About this time, his nose started to itch.

Soon after Zenchi had taken his nose out of the hot water, the young monk began to step on it with both feet. Zenchi rested on his side, watching the monk's feet go up and down.

Once in a while the young monk would feel sorry for Priest Zenchi. Looking down at Zenchi's head, he would say, "I hope it doesn't hurt. The doctor said to step hard on your nose. But I hope it doesn't hurt."

Zenchi tried to show that it didn't hurt by moving his head. But since his nose was being stepped on, it was not easy. Looking at the young monk's feet, he answered in a low voice, "It does not hurt so very much." Since it was the itchy part of his nose that was being stepped on, it felt quite good, in fact.

After a while, small oily bumps began to come out on Zenchi's nose. They made his nose look like the skin of a chicken after the feathers have been pulled out. Looking at this, the young monk stopped stepping on Zenchi's nose for a second and said, almost as if speaking to himself, "The doctor—he said they should be pulled out with tweezers."

Zenchi was not pleased, but he decided to leave the matter to the young monk. Zenchi understood that the young monk was being kind to him. But the fact that his nose was being viewed as a thing made him sad. Zenchi made a face to show his feelings, but he let the young monk go ahead and take out the oily bumps. The oil came out in little pieces that were about eleven millimeters long.

After all the bumps had been taken out, the young monk sighed and said, "We must put your nose into the hot water one more time."

Priest Zenchi made a difficult face, but he did as the young monk told him to do.

Then, after putting Zenchi's nose in hot water for the second time, they took it out once more. And what should they see but a nose that was shorter than ever before! Now it was not very different from a common nose that pointed down a little. As Zenchi touched his nose, the young monk handed him a mirror. But Zenchi was afraid to look into it.

Until now Zenchi's nose had hung down as far as his chin. That nose—that long, long nose—was now much smaller. It was not the nose that Zenchi had known for so many years. Now it hung down just as far as his upper lip. It was a little red here and there, in the places it had been stepped on. But no one would ever laugh at this nose, Zenchi thought. Finally, he looked into the mirror. The face in the mirror looked back at the face outside the mirror. Both faces looked happy.

The Nose

But that day was just one day, and Priest Zenchi worried that his nose would return to what it had been before. So he could not help touching the end of his nose when he was reading a sutra, or eating, or at other times. But his nose was not doing anything special. It was still hanging down to just above his upper lip, not any more than that. Zenchi soon went to bed. And the next morning, the first thing he did was to touch his nose to see if it had changed. It was still short, the same as yesterday. For the first time in many years, Priest Zenchi felt happy about life, just the way he felt after copying a sutra.

Over the next two or three days, Priest Zenchi discovered a fact that surprised him. A samurai came to the temple in Ike-no-o on business, as he had done before. This time he wore a strange look on his face, and without talking much, he looked again and again at Zenchi's nose. And that was not all. When Zenchi was walking outside and passed the boy monk who had dropped his nose into the bowl of rice, the boy and his young friends would first look down, then smile, and finally laugh out loud. And when Priest Zenchi gave orders to other monks, they wouldn't do anything strange while he was there, but as soon as Zenchi left, they would begin to laugh

The Nose

in low voices. This happened more than once.

At first, Priest Zenchi thought this was happening because his face had changed a little. Of course, that was one reason why the other monks laughed. But it could not be the only reason, because the way they laughed when his nose was long, and the way they laughed now, was different. The reason was simple: people don't laugh at things they see every day; they laugh at things they only see once in a while.

But this was not the only strange thing that was happening.

"They didn't laugh that way before. Why now?" Once in a while, when he had started to read a sutra out loud, Zenchi would stop and ask himself this question. At such times, Zenchi would look at the statue of Fugen Bodhisattva at his side and lose himself in thought. He thought of the time, just four or five days ago, when his nose was long. Those were the good old days. He could not help but feel sad. Zenchi did not know the answer to the question "Why now?"

The truth is, there are two different types of feeling in all men and women. First, we all feel sorry for a person who has had bad luck. But once that person is over his bad luck, then we begin to feel that we have lost something, something that was important. In a way, we would like to see the person have bad luck

The Nose

again. And before long, in a quiet kind of way, we begin to feel that, really, we do not like that person very much. Zenchi himself didn't know this yet, but he was beginning to get a feeling for it.

It was just at this point that Priest Zenchi began to feel out of step with life. Almost every chance he had, he would get angry and shout at someone. When Zenchi wasn't around, even the young monk who took care of his nose said, "It is wrong to do things like that, and Priest Zenchi will be sorry one day."

The one who especially made Zenchi angry was the boy monk who had dropped the Priest's nose into the bowl of rice. One day Zenchi heard the loud cry of a dog outside, and he went out to see what the problem was. He found the boy monk running after the dog with a piece of wood that was about sixty centimeters long. And that was not all. As he ran after the dog, the boy shouted, "Do you want a hit on the nose? Do you want a hit on the nose?" Without wasting a second, Zenchi took the piece of wood from the boy's hand, and with that same piece of wood, hit him in the face. It turned out that the piece of wood was the same one used to hold up Zenchi's nose.

Priest Zenchi came to think that his short nose was not, in every way, a good thing.

The Nose

Then, one night, something happened. After the sun had gone down, a strong wind came up, and Zenchi could hear the sounds of the wind from where he slept. It also got very cold, and Priest Zenchi was not able to sleep. As time passed, Zenchi's nose began to itch. Putting his hand to his nose, he could feel something like water. His nose had also gotten a little bigger, he thought. And it was hot, too.

"Maybe my nose is not well, because we did all those things to it to make it shorter," Priest Zenchi said to himself. At the same time he touched his nose, but he was very careful—as if he might break it.

The next morning, when Zenchi woke

early as he usually did, he found that the trees in the garden had dropped their leaves. The ground was all a gold color, the garden was filled with light, and there was bright ice on the building tops. Zenchi went outside, opened his mouth, and filled his body with fresh air.

It was then that he remembered a feeling that he had been trying to forget.

Suddenly he brought his hand up to his nose. What he felt was not the short nose he had felt yesterday. It was his old nose, the one that was fifteen to eighteen centimeters long and hung from above his upper lip down to his chin. Zenchi now knew that, in one night, his nose had returned to what it had been before. At the same time, he felt a song in his heart, the same wonderful feeling he had when his nose had first become short. Zenchi said to himself, "Now, no one will ever laugh at me again."

Then, as the sun rose in the sky, he let his long nose hang down from his face and play in the autumn wind.

In the Woods

山のふもとの藪の中で、男の死体が発見された。死んだ男に関する目撃証言や、事件関係者、被害者遺族、容疑者などの供述が次々と集まっていく。逮捕された盗人の男は、自分が男の妻に乱暴し、男を殺したのだという。死んだ男の妻は、自分が夫を刺し殺したのだという。そして、死んだ男自身男もまた、巫女の体を借りて自分が殺された顛末を語る。藪の中で、いったい何があったのか……。

読みはじめる前に

In the Woodsに出てくる語です。あらかじめ確認しておきましょう。

woodcutter	きこり
body	死体
suikan clothes	水干。平安・鎌倉時代の普段着で、通常、身頃の前後に補強のための総飾りがつく。
horse fly	アブ
sword	刀
Yamashina	京都市山科区
Sekiyama	関山。京都と滋賀の県境にある逢坂山を指す。関所が置かれていた。
bounty hunter	犯罪人の探索などに当たるべく雇われた前科者。
Tajomaru	(人名) 多襄丸
Awadaguchi	京都府東山区粟田口町。京都への東からの入り口にあたる。
palomino horse	月毛の馬。淡い金色の馬体を持つ。
Toribe Temple	鳥部寺。京都市東山区にあった。
Wakasa	若狭。現在の福井県西部。
Kanazawa Takehiro	(人名) 金沢武弘
Masago	(人名) 真砂。武弘の妻。
Kiyomizu Temple	清水寺
Bodhisattva Kanzeon	観世音菩薩
medium	霊媒師

The Woodcutter's Story

Yes, I am the one who found the body. This morning, as always, I went out to cut some wood. That is when I found the body in the woods at the foot of the hill.

Where exactly? About 450 meters from the Yamashina road. It's a place no one ever goes to. It is nothing but bamboo and some small cedar trees.

The body was on its back, looking up. He was wearing light-blue suikan clothes and a hat like you see in Kyoto. He was killed with one thrust of a sword to the chest. The bamboo leaves all around had blood on them. No, he wasn't bleeding when I found him. The wound had dried up. There was a horse fly sitting on his chest. It didn't even hear me coming.

Did I find a sword there? No, nothing like that. But there was a rope near the tree. And, oh yes, there was also a comb. That's all. But from the looks of the grass and bamboo leaves all around him, I would say that he put up quite a fight.

What? Was a horse there? No, no horse could get into a place like that. There is too much bamboo and too many trees. In any case, there is a horse path right near the woods.

The Traveling Monk's Story

Yes, I am sure that I saw the dead man yesterday on the Yamashina road. It was around noon. I was on my way from Sekiyama to Yamashina. The man was walking toward Sekiyama together with a woman on a horse. The woman's hat had a veil, so I couldn't see her face. The horse was a palomino. How tall was it? Well, I am a monk, you see, and don't really know much about such things. The man had a sword and a bow and set of arrows. I remember that quite well.

To think that he should come to this end. Well, I feel very sorry for him. That is all I can say.

The Bounty Hunter's Story

Are you asking about the person I caught? He is the one and only Tajomaru, the robber. I was lucky to catch him. He had been thrown from his horse, you see, and was moaning in pain on the bridge at Awataguchi.

The time? It was between seven and nine o'clock, last night. He was wearing dark-blue suikan clothes and carrying a sword, just as he was when I almost caught him once before. He also had a bow and a set of arrows.

In the Woods

You say the dead man was seen with the same bow and set of arrows? Then there is no mistake about it. It was Tajomaru who killed the man. Yes, he was riding a palomino horse. It was the same horse that you say the woman was riding. I found it near the bridge eating grass.

Tajomaru really likes women, much more than most of the robbers that work in Kyoto. He told me that he was the one who killed the mother and daughter near Toribe Temple last year. You must remember the case.

I have no idea what happened to the woman who was riding the palomino. Maybe you could look into that.

The Story of the Woman's Mother

Yes, the dead man was my daughter's husband. He was not from Kyoto. He was a samurai working in Wakasa. His name was Kanazawa Takehiro, and he was twenty-six years old. No, he was a kind man and not the type that anyone would want to hurt.

My daughter? Her name is Masago. She is nineteen. Her face is round and dark in color. She is a strong woman and knows what she wants. There was no man in her life before Takehiro. He was the first.

Yesterday she and Takehiro left for Wakasa. I never thought that such a thing could ever happen. But where is she now? Takehiro is dead, I know that. But I am worried about her. Oh, please find her for me, no matter what you have to do.

That terrible Tajomaru person, the robber. First Takehiro, then my daughter... (She breaks down crying.)

Tajomaru's Story

I killed the man, but not the woman. Where is she now? I don't know. You can start torturing me right now, but I can't tell you what I don't know. Now that I have been caught, I am going to tell you the true story.

Yesterday, a little after noon, I saw the two of them for the first time. Just as I was looking at the woman, the wind lifted the veil from her hat, and I saw her face. I saw it just for a second, but that second made all the difference. It was a face from another world. I decided right then that I would get that woman, even if I had to kill the man.

It is not as difficult as you think to kill a man. And if I really wanted to get the woman, then the man must die. Still, if I could get the woman without killing the man, that was all right, too. In fact, at the time I thought I could do just that. Of course, I couldn't do it out on the Yamashina road. That is when I thought of a way to get them off the road and into the woods.

This is what I did. As I walked along with them, I said that I had discovered some hidden treasure and wanted to sell it cheap. The treasure was now in the woods at the foot of the hill. I could show them if they were interested.

The man was interested from the beginning, and the more I talked about it, the more interested he got. It's true—if someone really wants something, you can make them do whatever you want. So the three of us set off toward the hill and the woods—me, the man, and the woman on the horse.

We reached the foot of the hill, and the man was all ready to go into the woods and see the treasure. But the woman stayed on her horse and said that she would wait there. That wasn't surprising, since the woods had so much bamboo and so many cedar trees. In fact, I was glad that she decided not to come along. That way, I could be alone with the man.

At first, the woods is all bamboo. But along the way there is an open space with some cedar trees. You couldn't find a better place for my kind of work. I told the man that the treasure was buried at the foot of one of the trees. He believed me and moved toward the cedars as fast as he could. Then, just as we got near the trees, I grabbed him and threw him down. He had a sword and he was strong. But I caught him by surprise, and before you knew it I had him tied to one of the cedars.

Where did I get the rope? Well, a rope is a robber's best friend. We always carry one, just in case. And to keep him from crying out, I pushed some bamboo leaves into his mouth. It was as easy as that.

After I took care of the man, I went back to where the woman was and told her that the man was feeling sick. This went exactly as planned, and she agreed to go see what was wrong. She took off her hat, and I took her by the hand and led her into the woods.

When we got near the trees, she saw the man tied to the cedar. Before I knew it, she was holding a dagger in her hand. I have never seen a woman so ready to fight. If I hadn't been careful, she would have stabbed me, just like that.

But you must not forget that I am

Tajomaru, not just some man you see walking down the road. Without using my sword, I finally got the dagger out of her hand. And without the dagger, there was not much she could do. So this is how I had my way with the woman without killing the man.

Yes, I said that I had my way with the woman without killing the man. In fact, I had never planned to kill the man. The woman was crying when I started to leave the woods, and she grabbed my arm to stop me. At first, it was hard to understand what she was saying. But then I understood. She said that either I must die or her husband must die. Both of us had seen her shamed, and she couldn't live with both of us alive. One of us must die. She would go with the one who was left alive. That is when, suddenly, I wanted very much to kill the man. (Tajomaru has a dark, excited look on his face.)

I am less human than you. That is what you are thinking. I know. But you did not see the woman's face. You did not see the fire in her eyes when she grabbed my arm. When I looked into those eyes, I knew that I must have her as my wife. Yes, I must have her as my wife.

You think that I wanted only her body, nothing more. But no, I had already had my way with her body. I could have just left her in the woods with her husband, and her husband's blood would not be on my sword. But the second I looked into her eyes, I knew I could not leave those dark woods without first killing her husband.

But if I had to kill him, I wanted to do it in the right way, like a man. So I took off the rope and gave him his sword. (I forgot to take the rope with me and left it near the tree.) The man had a terrible look on his face. Without saying a word, he came straight at me. It was the hardest fight I have ever fought. It was finally the twenty-third thrust of my sword that went through his chest. The twenty-third thrust! Remember that. I will never forget it. Never have I fought a man that long and hard. (He smiles.)

As soon as the man fell, I put away my sword and turned toward the woman. And what did I see? The woman was gone. I looked for her among the trees. I looked at the leaves on the ground for some sign of where she had gone. I listened for a sound, but the only sound I heard was the man's dying breath.

Maybe she left the woods and went for help as soon as the fight started. If that was true, then I was in danger. Without wasting any more time, I picked up the man's sword, his bow, and the set of arrows and left the woods. The woman's horse was still outside the woods.

There is no need to say more. I can say, though, that I no longer had the man's sword before coming back to Kyoto.

This is the end of my story, and the end of my life. Do with me as you please. (He looks straight ahead.)

The Story of a Woman at Kiyomizu Temple

After the robber in dark-blue suikan clothes had his way with me, he looked down at my husband and laughed. How terrible my husband must have felt! I ran to where he was. Or I should say that I tried to. The robber was quick to stop me and throw me to the ground.

That is when I saw something in my husband's eyes. My husband wasn't able to speak because of the leaves in his mouth, but everything he wanted to say was in his eyes. His eyes showed that he was not angry at me or sad; they showed that he looked down on me—he despised me. I had felt some pain when the robber threw me to the ground, but when my husband looked at me with those eyes, it broke my heart. Without knowing what I was doing, I cried out, then fainted and fell to the ground.

When I finally woke, the robber was gone. There was only my husband, still tied to the cedar tree. I got up from the ground and looked at my husband's face. His eyes had not changed. They showed that he still despised me, that he looked down on me, that he even hated me. I don't know how to explain how I felt—shamed, sad, angry. It was difficult for me to walk, but still, I went to him.

"With all that has happened," I said, "we can no longer be husband and wife. I am prepared to die, but I must ask that you also be prepared to die. You have seen me shamed, and I cannot let you go on living after that."

After I had finished speaking, my husband looked at me as if I was not human. I felt a terrible pain in my chest, but I started looking for my husband's sword all the same. I couldn't find it or the bow and set of arrows. The robber must have taken them. But I did find my dagger. As I took the dagger and raised it above my head, I said to my husband, "I must ask for your life. I will follow soon after."

Hearing this, my husband tried to speak for the first time, but I couldn't understand him. I couldn't understand, but I knew in my heart. What he wanted to say was, "Kill me!" I felt as if I were in a dream, but still, with one thrust of the dagger, I stabbed him hard in the chest.

At this point I must have fainted again. When I woke and looked around, my husband was still tied to the tree, but now he was dead. Through the leaves of the bamboo and cedar trees, some light from the setting sun fell on his face. I was crying when I took the rope off his body and threw it away.

And then...what happened to me

then? I really don't know. But I can tell you that I didn't have what it takes to kill myself. I tried stabbing myself; I tried throwing myself into a pond. But still I couldn't die. I wish I had. (She smiles in a sad way.) Even the Bodhisattva Kanzeon would not be sorry for someone like me. But what am I to do? The robber had his way with me, and then I killed my own husband. What am I to do? (She suddenly breaks down and cries.)

The Dead Husband's Story Told through a Medium

After the robber had his way with my wife, he sat down next to her and tried to make her think that it was all for the best. Of course, I was not able to say a word, and I was still tied to the tree. But I tried to tell her with my eyes that she shouldn't believe a word the robber said. But she just sat on the ground, looking down. I think she was listening to what the robber said. I wished I was in his place and able to talk to her like that.

In the Woods

The robber was clever in the way he spoke. He explained to her that once a woman has been shamed, she can never get along with her husband in the same way as before. It would be better, he said, if she came along with him. He told her that it was because he liked her so much that he had done what he had done. The robber was clever. He would say anything to get what he wanted.

After she had finished listening to the robber's sweet words, she looked up with a special look on her face, almost as if she had eaten something very delicious. I have never, ever, seen my wife look as beautiful as she looked then.

But then she gave her answer to the

robber, and I will never forget what she said. "Take me with you, no matter where you go." (He says nothing more for a long while.)

This is not the only wrong my wife did to me. If that were the only wrong, I would not continue to suffer as I do now. The robber took her hand and started to lead her out of the woods. She stopped and turned toward him. All color was gone from her face. She pointed at me and cried out, "Kill him! I cannot go with you while he is alive."

She shouted this over and over. "Please kill him! Please kill him!" It was like a heavy rain pounding on my body, pushing me down into the dark of night. Were such terrible words ever spoken before? (He stops and smiles in a strange way.) Even the robber couldn't believe his ears.

As she shouted these words, she grabbed the robber's arm and held on to him. He just looked at her. He didn't say if he would kill me or not. He just looked at her. Then, before you knew it, he had kicked her down onto the ground. (He stops again and smiles in a strange way.) The robber's eyes were hard when he turned to look at me. "What do you want me to do with this woman? Kill her or let her go? Just nod if you want me to kill her." For these words alone, I was ready to forget all the robber had done to me.

As my wife was waiting for my

answer, she suddenly let out a cry and ran toward the deep part of the woods. The robber tried to catch her, but she got away. I just sat there. It was like watching a scene from a strange dream.

The robber came back without her and picked up the sword and the bow and arrows. He cut my rope in one place. As he left the woods, I thought I heard him say, "Now I am the one in danger." After that, all was quiet. As I took the rope from around my body, I listened for any sounds. I thought I heard something, but it was only my own voice crying. (For the third time, he stops speaking.)

While it was not easy, I finally got to my feet. On the ground in front of me,

In the Woods

I saw my wife's dagger, catching the last light of the sun. I picked it up and held it in my hand. Then, in one quick move, I thrust it into my chest. In my mouth, there was suddenly the taste of blood. But I didn't feel any pain. My chest began to turn cold, and all around me grew very quiet. Ah, so quiet! Not even one small bird sang its song in these woods. There was only the dark air around the bamboo and cedar trees. I, too, was pulled deeper into that dark.

As the air grew close around me, I heard someone coming. I tried to look and see who it was, but I could not see through the dark cloud. Then a hand—a hand I could not see—pulled the dagger from my chest. In my mouth, the taste of blood grew stronger. Then I began the long, long fall into the deep, dark night.

Word List

- LEVEL 1, 2は本文で使われている全ての語を掲載しています。
  LEVEL 3以上は、中学校レベルの語を含みません。ただし、本文で特殊な意味で使われている場合、その意味のみを掲載しています。
- 語形が規則変化する語の見出しは原形で示しています。不規則変化語は本文中で使われている形になっています。
- 一般的な意味を紹介していますので、一部の語で本文で実際に使われている品詞や意味と合っていないことがあります。
- 品詞は以下のように示しています。

名 名詞	代 代名詞	形 形容詞	副 副詞	動 動詞	助 助動詞
前 前置詞	接 接続詞	間 間投詞	冠 冠詞	略 略語	俗 俗語
熟 熟語	頭 接頭語	尾 接尾語	号 記号	関 関係代名詞	

A

- **a** 冠 ①1つの, 1人の, ある ②〜につき
- **able** 形 ①《be-to〜》(人が)〜することができる ②能力のある
- **about** 副 ①およそ, 約 ②まわりに, あたりを 前 ①〜について ②〜のまわりに[の]
- **above** 前 ①〜の上に ②〜より上で, 〜以上で ③〜を超えて
- **across** 前 〜を渡って, 〜の向こう側に, (身体の一部に)かけて
- **afraid** 形 ①心配して ②恐れて, こわがって
- **after** 前 ①〜の後に[で], 〜の次に ②《前後に名詞がきて》次々に〜, 何度も〜《反復・継続を表す》 **after a while** しばらくして **after all** やはり, 結局 **after that** その後 **one after another** 次々に, 1つ[人]ずつ **run after** 〜を追いかける 副 後に[で] 接 (〜した)後に[で]
- **again** 副 再び, もう一度 **again and again** 何度も繰り返して
- **against** 前 ①〜に対して, 〜に反対して, (規則など)に違反して ②〜にもたれて
- **ago** 副 〜前に

- **agree** 動 ①同意する ②意見が一致する
- **ah** 間 《驚き・悲しみ・賞賛などを表して》ああ, やっぱり
- **ahead** 副 前方へ[に] **go ahead** (仕事を)続ける **look straight ahead** まっすぐ前を見る
- **air** 名 ①《the-》空中, 空間 ②空気, 《the-》大気 **the air grow close** 空気がもやがかる, 薄闇が立ち込める
- **alive** 形 ①生きている ②活気のある, 生き生きとした
- **all** 形 すべての, 〜中 **all the way** ずっと, はるばる, いろいろと 代 全部, すべて(のもの[人]) **after all** やはり, 結局 **all for the best** 万事うまくいって, 結果オーライで **first of all** まず第一に **with all** 〜がありながら 名 全体 **all right** 大丈夫で, よろしい, 申し分ない, わかった, 承知した **all the same** とにかく, いずれにせよ **not 〜 at all** 少しも[全然]〜ない 副 まったく, すっかり **all at once** 突然, 出し抜けに
- **almost** 副 ほとんど, もう少しで(〜するところ)
- **alone** 形 ただひとりの **alone with** 〜と2人だけで 副 ひとりで, 〜だけで
- **along** 前 〜に沿って **along the**

Word List

way 途中で, これまでに, この先 副 ～に沿って, 前へ, 進んで **along with** ～と一緒に **come along** 一緒に来る, ついて来る **get along with** (人)と仲良くする, 気(うま)が合う, 歩調を合わせる **walk along** (前へ)歩く, ～に沿って歩く

☐ **already** 副 すでに, もう

☐ **also** 副 ～も(また), ～も同様に

☐ **always** 副 いつも, 常に **as always** いつものように

☐ **am** 動 ～である, (～に)いる[ある]《主語がIのときのbeの現在形》

☐ **among** 前 (3つ以上のもの)の間で[に], ～の中で[に]

☐ **an** 冠 ①1つの, 1人の, ある ②～につき

☐ **and** 接 ①そして, ～と… ②《同じ語を結んで》ますます ③《結果を表して》それで, だから

☐ **anger** 名 怒り

☐ **angry** 形 怒って, 腹を立てて **be angry at** ～に腹を立てている **get angry** 腹を立てる

☐ **another** 形 ①もう1つ[1人]の ②別の 代 ①もう1つ[1人] ②別のもの **one after another** 次々に, 1つ[人]ずつ **one another** お互い

☐ **answer** 動 ①答える, 応じる ②《–for ～》～の責任を負う 名 答え, 応答, 返事

☐ **any** 形 ①《疑問文で》何か, いくつかの ②《否定文で》何も, 少しも(～ない) ③《肯定文で》どの～も **in any case** いずれにせよ, とにかく **not any more than** ～より上にはならない 代 ①《疑問文で》(～のうち)何か, どれか, 誰か ②《否定文で》少しも, 何[誰]も[～ない] ③《肯定文で》どれも, 誰でも

☐ **anymore** 副 《通例否定文, 疑問文で》今はもう, これ以上, これから

☐ **anyone** 代 ①《疑問文・条件節で》誰か ②《否定文で》誰も(～ない) ③《肯定文で》誰でも

☐ **anything** 代 ①《疑問文で》何か, どれでも ②《否定文で》何も, どれも(～ない) ③《肯定文で》何でも, どれでも 副 いくらか

☐ **appear** 動 ①現れる, 見えてくる ②(～のように)見える, ～らしい

☐ **are** 動 ～である, (～に)いる[ある]《主語がyou, we, theyまたは複数名詞のときのbeの現在形》名 アール《面積単位。100平方メートル》

☐ **arm** 名 腕

☐ **armor** 名 よろい, かぶと, 甲冑

☐ **around** 副 ①まわりに, あちこちに ②およそ, 約 **look around** まわりを見回す 前 ～のまわりに, ～のあちこちに

☐ **arrow** 名 矢, 矢のようなもの

☐ **as** 接 ①《as ～ as …の形で》…と同じくらい～ ②～のとおりに, ～のように ③～しながら, ～しているときに ④～するにつれて, ～にしたがって ⑤～なので ⑥～だけれども ⑦～する限りでは 前 ①～として ②～の時 副 同じくらい 代 ①～のような ②～だが **as always** いつものように **as far as** ～と同じくらい遠く, ～まで, ～する限り(では) **as if** あたかも～のように, まるで～みたいに **as long as** ～する以上は, ～である限りは **as soon as** ～するとすぐ, ～するや否や **as well** なお, その上, 同様に **as ～ as one can** できる限り～ **be known as** ～として知られている **just as** (ちょうど)であろうとおり **see ～ as** …を…と考える **such as** たとえば～, ～のような **the same ～ as** …と同じ(ような)～

☐ **ask** 動 ①尋ねる, 聞く ②頼む, 求める **ask for** ～を要求する

☐ **at** 前 ①《場所・時》～に[で] ②《目標・方向》～に[を], ～に向かって ③《原因・理由》～を見て[聞いて・知って] ④～に従事して, ～の状態で **at first** 最初は, 初めのうちは **at once** すぐに, 同時に **at the foot of** ～のすそ[下部]に **at the time** そのころ, 当時は **at this point** 現在のところ

☐ **autumn** 名 秋

Short Stories of Ryunosuke Akutagawa

- **Awataguchi** 粟田口《地名。京都市》
- **away** 副 離れて, 遠くに, 去って, わ
  get away 逃げる, 逃亡する, 離れる
  keep away from ～に近寄らない
  put away 片づける, 取っておく
  right away すぐに
  throw away ～を捨てる；～を無駄に費やす, 浪費する
  walk away 立ち去る, 遠ざかる
  形 離れた

B

- **back** 名 ①背中 ②裏, 後ろ on one's back あおむけに 副 ①戻って ②後ろへ[に] come back 戻る come back to ～へ帰ってくる, ～に戻る go back to ～に帰る[戻る] look back at ～に視線を戻す, ～を振り返って見る
- **bad** 形 ①悪い, へたな, まずい ②気の毒な ③(程度が)ひどい, 激しい bad luck 災難, 不運, 悪運 That's too bad. 残念だ。
- **ball** 名 ボール, 球
- **bamboo** 名 竹(類), 竹材 形 竹の
- **bat** 名 コウモリ
- **bath** 名 入浴, 水浴, 風呂 bath house 湯屋
- **be** 動 ～である, (～に)いる[ある], ～となる 助 ①《現在分詞とともに用いて》～している ②《過去分詞とともに用いて》～される, ～されている
- **beautiful** 形 美しい, すばらしい
- **became** 動 become (なる)の過去
- **because** 接 (なぜなら)～だから, ～という理由[原因]で because of ～のために, ～の理由で
- **become** 動 ①(～に)なる ②(～に)似合う ③become の過去分詞
- **bed** 名 ベッド, 寝所 go to bed 床につく, 寝る
- **been** 動 be (～である)の過去分詞 助 be (～している・～される)の過去分詞
- **before** 前 ～の前に[で], ～より以前に before long やがて, まもなく 接 ～する前に before you know it あっという間に, 驚くほど早く 副 以前に
- **began** 動 begin (始まる)の過去
- **begin** 動 始まる[始める], 起こる
- **beginning** 名 初め, 始まり
- **begun** 動 begin (始まる)の過去分詞
- **behind** 前 ①～の後ろに, ～の背後に ②～に遅れて, ～に劣って leave behind あとにする, ～を置き去りにする 副 ①後ろに, 背後に ②遅れて, 劣って
- **being** 名 存在, 生命, 人間 human being 人, 人間
- **believe** 動 信じる, 信じている, (～と)思う, 考える
- **below** 前 ①～より下に ②～以下の, ～より劣る 副 下に[へ]
- **best** 形 最もよい, 最大[多]の try one's best 全力を尽くす 名 《the -》①最上のもの ②全力, 精いっぱい all for the best 万事うまくいって, 結果オーライで
- **better** 形 ①よりよい ②(人が)回復して
- **between** 前 (2つのもの)の間に[で・の]
- **big** 形 ①大きい ②偉い, 重要な
- **bird** 名 鳥
- **black** 形 黒い, 有色の
- **bleed** 動 出血する, 血を流す[流させる]
- **blood** 名 血, 血液
- **blow** 動 (風が)吹く, (風が)～を吹き飛ばす
- **blue** 形 青い 名 青(色)
- **Bodhisattva** 名 菩薩
- **Bodhisattva Kanzeon** 観世音菩薩, 観音様
- **body** 名 体, 死体, 胴体

Word List

- **book** 名 本, 書物
- **born** 動 be born 生まれる 形 生まれた, 生まれながらの
- **both** 形 両方の, 2つともの 代 両方, 両者, 双方 both of them 彼ら[それら]両方とも
- **bought** 動 buy (買う) の過去, 過去分詞
- **bounty hunter** 賞金稼ぎ
- **bow** 名 弓, 弓状のもの
- **bowl** 名 どんぶり, わん, ボウル
- **boy** 名 少年, 男の子
- **break** 動 ①壊す, 折る ②(記録・法律・約束を)破る ③中断する break down 泣き崩れず, 取り乱す break out 発生する, 急に起こる
- **breath** 名 ①息, 呼吸 ②《a-》(風の)そよぎ, 気配, きざし
- **bridge** 名 橋
- **bright** 形 ①輝いている, 鮮明な ②快活な ③利口な
- **bring** 動 ①持ってくる, 連れてくる ②もたらす, 生じる bring up (問題を)持ち出す
- **broke** 動 break (壊す)の過去
- **brought** 動 bring (持ってくる)の過去, 過去分詞
- **building** 名 建物, 建造物, ビルディング
- **bump** 名 こぶ, 隆起 oily bump 角栓, 皮脂の固まり
- **buried** 動 bury (埋める)の過去, 過去分詞
- **burn** 動 燃える, 燃やす
- **burning** 形 燃えている, 燃えるように暑い
- **bury** 動 ①埋葬する, 埋める ②覆い隠す
- **business** 名 ①職業, 仕事 ②商売 ③用事 on business 仕事で
- **but** 接 ①でも, しかし ②〜を除いて but still それにしても not 〜 but … 〜ではなくて… nothing but ただ〜だけ, 〜にすぎない, 〜のほかは何も…ない 前 〜を除いて, 〜のほかは 副 ただ, のみ, ほんの
- **by** 前 ①《位置》〜のそばに[で] ②《手段・方法・行為者・基準》〜によって, 〜で ③《期限》〜までには ④《通過・経由》〜を経由して, 〜を通って by oneself 一人で, 自分だけで, 独力で take someone by the hand (人の)手を取る[引く] 副 そばに, 通り過ぎて stand by そばに立つ, 傍観する, 待機する stop by 途中で立ち寄る, ちょっと訪ねる

C

- **call** 動 呼ぶ, 叫ぶ
- **came** 動 come (来る)の過去
- **can** 助 ①〜できる ②〜してもよい ③〜でありうる ④《否定文で》〜のはずがない as 〜 as one can できる限り〜 cannot help 〜ing 〜せずにはいられない
- **capital** 名 首都
- **care** 名 ①心配, 注意 ②世話, 介護 take care of 〜の世話をする, 〜面倒を見る, 〜を管理する
- **careful** 形 注意深い, 慎重な
- **carry** 動 ①運ぶ, 連れていく, 持ち歩く ②伝わる, 伝える
- **cart** 名 荷馬車, 荷車
- **case** 名 ①事件, 問題, 事柄 ②実例, 場合 ③実状, 状況, 症状 ④箱 in any case とにかく in case 〜だといけないので, 念のため, 万が一
- **catch** 動 ①つかまえる ②追いつく ③(病気に)かかる catch someone by surprise 不意打ちをかける, 不意をつく
- **caught** 動 catch (つかまえる)の過去, 過去分詞
- **cause** 動 (〜の)原因となる, 引き起こす
- **cedar** 名 ヒマラヤスギ, レバノン杉

Short Stories of Ryunosuke Akutagawa

- □ **cent** 名セント《米国などの通貨単位。1ドルの100分の1》
- □ **center** 名①中心, 中央 ②中心地[人物] 動集中する[させる]
- □ **centimeter** 名センチメートル《長さの単位》
- □ **chance** 名①偶然, 運 ②好機 ③見込み
- □ **change** 動①変わる, 変える ②交換する 名①変化, 変更 ②取り替え, 乗り換え
- □ **cheap** 副安く
- □ **chest** 名胸, 肺
- □ **chicken** 名ニワトリ(鶏)
- □ **chin** 名あご
- □ **China** 名中国
- □ **Chinese** 形中国(人)の
- □ **Chorakuji Temple** 名長楽寺
- □ **city** 名都市
- □ **clever** 形頭のよい, 利口な
- □ **close** 形①近い ②親しい ③狭い **be close to** ~に近い 副①接近して ②密集して **the air grow close** 空気がもやがかる, 薄闇が立ち込める 動①閉まる, 閉める ②終える, 閉店する
- □ **clothes** 名衣服, 身につけるもの
- □ **clothing** 名衣類, 衣料品
- □ **cloud** 名雲, 雲状のもの
- □ **cold** 形寒い, 冷たい
- □ **color** 名色, 色彩
- □ **comb** 名くし
- □ **come** 動①来る, 行く, 現れる ②(出来事が)起こる, 生じる ③~になる ④comeの過去分詞 **come along** 一緒に来る, ついて来る **come around** ぐるっと回ってやってくる **come back** 戻る **come back to** ~へ帰ってくる, ~に戻る **come down** 下りて来る **come out** 出てくる, 姿を現す **come through** 通り抜ける, 成功する, 期待に沿う **come to** (良くない状態に)なってしまう **come up** 発生する
- □ **coming** 形今度の, 来たるべき
- □ **common** 形①共通の, 共同の ②普通の, 平凡な ③一般の, 公共の
- □ **continue** 動続く, 続ける, (中断後)再開する, (ある方向に)移動していく
- □ **copy** 動写す, まねる
- □ **could** 助①can(~できる)の過去 ②《控え目な推量・可能性・願望などを表す》**could have done** ~だったかもしれない《仮定法》 **If** +《主語》+ **could** ~できればなあ《仮定法》
- □ **course** 名《of course》もちろん, 当然
- □ **creature** 名生物, 動物
- □ **cry** 動泣く, 叫ぶ, 大声を出す, 嘆く **cry out** 叫ぶ 名①泣き声, 叫び, かっさい
- □ **cut** 動①切る, 刈る ②短縮する, 削る ③cutの過去, 過去分詞 **cut through** 切り開く

D

- □ **dagger** 名短剣
- □ **dance** 動踊る, ダンスをする
- □ **danger** 名危険, 障害, 脅威
- □ **dark** 形①暗い, 闇の ②(色が)濃い, (髪が)黒い 名①《the -》暗がり, 闇 ②日暮れ, 夜 ③暗い色[影]
- □ **dark-blue** 形紺色の
- □ **daughter** 名娘
- □ **day** 名①日中, 昼間 ②日, 期日 ③《-s》時代, 生涯 **day and night** 昼も夜も **every day** 毎日 **from day to day** その日その日で **one day** (過去の)ある日, (未来の)いつか
- □ **dead** 形①死んでいる, 活気のない, 枯れた ②まったくの
- □ **decide** 動決定[決意]する, (~しようと)決める, 判決を下す
- □ **deep** 形①深い, 深さ~の ②深遠な ③濃い

Word List

- **delicious** 形 おいしい, うまい
- **demon** 名 悪魔 **demon warrior** 神将
- **desk** 名 机, 台
- **despise** 動 軽蔑する
- **devil** 名 悪魔 (のような人), 鬼
- **did** 動 do (〜をする)の過去 助 do の過去
- **die** 動 死ぬ, 消滅する
- **difference** 名 違い, 相違, 差 **make all the difference** 状況を一変させる
- **different** 形 異なった, 違った, 別の, さまざまな **be different from** 〜と違う
- **difficult** 形 困難な, むずかしい, 扱いにくい
- **dig** 動 掘る
- **dinner** 名 ディナー, 夕食
- **disappear** 動 見えなくなる, 姿を消す, なくなる
- **discover** 動 発見する, 気づく
- **do** 動 ①《ほかの動詞とともに用いて現在形の否定文・疑問文をつくる》②《同じ動詞を繰り返す代わりに用いる》③《動詞を強調するのに用いる》動 〜をする **do just that** その通りにやる **do with** 〜を処理する, 〜をどうにかする
- **doctor** 名 医者
- **does** 動 do (〜をする)の3人称単数現在 助 do の3人称単数現在
- **dog** 名 犬
- **done** 動 do (〜をする)の過去分詞
- **Dotei Lake** 洞庭湖
- **down** 副 ①上へ, 降りて, 低くなって ②倒れて **up and down** 上がったり下がったり, 行ったり来たり, あちこちと 前 〜の下方へ, 〜を下って **walk down** 〜を歩く[歩いていく]
- **dragon** 名 竜
- **dream** 名 夢, 幻想
- **dress** 動 服を着る[着せる]

- **dried** 動 dry (乾燥する)の過去, 過去分詞
- **drink** 動 飲む, 飲酒する
- **drive** 動 追いやる, (ある状態に)する
- **drop** 動 ①(ぽたぽた)落ちる, 落とす ②下がる, 下げる
- **drum** 名 太鼓, ドラム
- **dry** 動 乾燥する **dry up** すっかり乾く
- **dug** 動 dig (掘る)の過去, 過去分詞
- **dying** 形 死にかかっている, 消えそうな

E

- **each** 形 それぞれの, 各自の **each other** お互いに 代 それぞれ, 各自 副 それぞれに
- **ear** 名 耳, 聴覚
- **early** 副 早く, 早めに
- **earring** 名《通例-s》イヤリング
- **earth** 名 ①《the –》地球 ②大地, 陸地, 土 ③この世 **the face of the earth** 地球全体
- **easy** 形 ①やさしい, 簡単な ②気楽な, くつろいだ
- **eat** 動 食べる, 食事する
- **eaten** 動 eat (食べる)の過去分詞
- **eighteen** 名 18(の数字), 18人[個] 形 18の, 18人[個]の
- **either** 形 ①(2つのうち)どちらかの ②どちらでも 代 どちらも, どちらでも 副 ①どちらか ②《否定文で》〜もまた(…ない) 接《- 〜 or …》〜かまたは…か
- **eleven** 名 ①11(の数字), 11人[個] ②11人のチーム, イレブン 形 11の, 11人[個]の
- **emperor** 名 皇帝, 天皇
- **end** 名 ①終わり, 終末, 死 ②果て, 末, 端 ③目的 動 終わる, 終える

- [ ] **enormous** 形 ばく大な, 非常に大きい, 巨大な
- [ ] **enough** 形 十分な, (~するのに)足る **enough to do** ~するのに十分な
- [ ] **especially** 副 特別に, とりわけ
- [ ] **even** 副 ①《強意》~でさえも, ~ですら, いっそう, なおさら ②平等に **even if** たとえ~でも 形 ①平らな, 水平の ②等しい, 均一の ③落ち着いた
- [ ] **evening** 名 ①夕方, 晩 《the [one's] –》末期, 晩年, 衰退期
- [ ] **ever** 副 ①今までに, これまで, かつて, いつまでも ②《強意》いったい **ever since** それ以来ずっと **never ever** 絶対に, 決して
- [ ] **every** 形 ①どの~も, すべての, あらゆる ②毎~, ~ごとの **every day** 毎日
- [ ] **everything** 代 すべてのこと[もの], 何でも, 何もかも
- [ ] **everywhere** 副 どこにいても, いたるところに
- [ ] **evil** 形 ①邪悪な ②有害な, 不吉な **evil spirit** 魔性
- [ ] **exactly** 副 ①正確に, 厳密に, ちょうど ②まったくそのとおり
- [ ] **example** 名 例, 見本, 模範 **for example** たとえば
- [ ] **excited** 形 興奮した, わくわくした
- [ ] **expensive** 形 高価な, ぜいたくな
- [ ] **experience** 名 経験, 体験
- [ ] **explain** 動 説明する, 明らかにする, 釈明[弁明]する
- [ ] **eye** 名 目

F

- [ ] **face** 名 ①顔, 顔つき ②外観, 外見 **the face of the earth** 地球全体
- [ ] **fact** 名 事実, 真相 **in fact** つまり, 実は, 要するに
- [ ] **faint** 動 気絶する
- [ ] **fall** 動 ①落ちる, 倒れる ②(値段・温度が)下がる ③(ある状態に)急に陥る **fall down** 落ちる, 転ぶ **fall into** ~に陥る, ~してしまう **fall on** ~に降りかかる **fall to the ground** 転ぶ
- [ ] **fallen** 動 fall (落ちる) の過去分詞
- [ ] **far** 副 ①遠くに, はるかに, 離れて ②《比較級を強めて》ずっと, はるかに 形 遠い, 向こうの **as far as** ~と同じくらい遠く, ~まで, ~する限り(では)
- [ ] **fast** 形 (速度が)速い
- [ ] **father** 名 父親
- [ ] **feather** 名 羽, 《-s》羽毛
- [ ] **feel** 動 感じる, (~と)思う **feel sick** 気分が悪い **feel sorry for** ~をかわいそうに思う
- [ ] **feeling** 名 ①感じ, 気持ち ②触感, 知覚 ③同情, 思いやり, 感受性
- [ ] **feet** 名 ①foot (足) の複数 ②フィート《長さの単位: 約30cm》 **get to one's feet** 立ち上がる **to one's feet** 両足で立っている状態
- [ ] **fell** 動 fall (落ちる) の過去
- [ ] **felt** 動 feel (感じる) の過去, 過去分詞
- [ ] **field** 名 野原, 田畑, 広がり
- [ ] **fifteen** 名 15 (の数字), 15人[個] 形 15の, 15人[個]の
- [ ] **fifty** 名 50 (の数字), 50人[個] 形 50の, 50人[個]の
- [ ] **fight** 動 (~と)戦う, 争う 名 ①戦い, 争い, けんか ②闘志, ファイト **put up a fight** 戦う, 抵抗する
- [ ] **fill** 動 ①満ちる, 満たす ②《be -ed with ~》~でいっぱいである
- [ ] **finally** 副 最後に, ついに, 結局
- [ ] **find** 動 ①見つける ②(~と)わかる, 気づく, ~と考える ③得る
- [ ] **fine** 形 美しい, りっぱな, 申し分ない, 結構な
- [ ] **finger** 名 (手の)指 動 ~を指でいじる

Word List

- **finish** 動 終わる, 終える finish doing ~するのを終える
- **fire** 名 火, 炎, 火事
- **first** 名 最初, 第一 (の人・物) at first 最初は, 初めのうちは first of all まず第一に 形 ①第一の, 最初の ②最も重要な for the first time 初めて 副 第一に, 最初に
- **five** 名 5 (の数字), 5人[個] 形 5の, 5人[個] の
- **flew** 動 fly (飛ぶ) の過去
- **flicker** 動 (灯などが) 明滅する, ちらちら (揺れて) 見える
- **fly** 動 ①飛ぶ, 飛ばす ②飛ぶように) 過ぎる, 急ぐ fly off 飛び去る 名 ①飛行 ②ハエ horse fly アブ
- **follow** 動 ①ついていく, あとをたどる ②(~の) 結果として起こる ③(忠告などに) 従う ④理解できる
- **follower** 名 信奉者, 追随者, 弟子
- **foot** 名 ①足, 足取り ②(山などの) ふもと, (物の) 最下部, すそ ③フィート《長さの単位, 約30cm》 at the foot of ~のすそ[下部]に
- **for** 前 ①《目的・原因・対象》~にとって, ~のために[の], ~に対して ②《期間》~間 ③《代理》~の代わりに ④《方向》~へ (向かって) for a while しばらくの間, 少しの間 for ~ alone ~だけを取っても, ~のために for example たとえば for long 長い間 for oneself 独力で, 自分のために for the first time 初めて for ~ years ~年間, ~年にわたって 接 というわけは~, なぜなら~, だから
- **forget** 動 忘れる, 置き忘れる forget to do ~することを忘れる
- **forgot** 動 forget (忘れる) の過去, 過去分詞
- **fought** 動 fight (戦う) の過去, 過去分詞
- **found** 動 ①find (見つける) の過去, 過去分詞
- **four** 名 4 (の数字), 4人[個] 形 4の, 4人[個] の

- **fresh** 形 ①新鮮な, 生気のある ②さわやかな, 清純な ③新規の
- **friend** 名 友だち, 仲間
- **friendly** 形 親しみのある, 親切な, 友情のこもった
- **from** 前 ①《出身・出発点・時間・順序・原料》~から ②《原因・理由》~がもとで
- **front** 名 正面, 前 in front of ~の前に, ~の正面に 形 正面の, 前面の
- **Fugen Bodhisattva** 普賢菩薩

G

- **Gabisan, Mt.** 峨眉山
- **Gakuyo Town** 岳陽《街の名》
- **game** 名 ゲーム, 試合, 遊び, 競技
- **garden** 名 庭, 庭園
- **gate** 名 門, 扉, 入り口
- **gave** 動 give (与える) の過去
- **get** 動 ①得る, 手に入れる ②(ある状態に) なる, いたる ③わかる, 理解する ④~させる, ~を (…の状態に) する ⑤(ある場所に) 達する, 着く get along with (人) と仲良くする, 気[うま]が合う, 歩調を合わせる get angry 腹を立てる get away 逃げる, 逃亡する, 離れる get into ~に入る, 入り込む get near 接近する get off ~を…から離す get on (電車などに) 乗る get ready 用意[支度] をする get someone to do (人) に~させる[してもらう] get to one's feet 立ち上がる get up 起き上がる, 立ち上がる
- **give** 動 ①与える, 贈る ②伝える, 述べる ③(~を) する give way 道を譲る, 譲歩する
- **given** 動 give (与える) の過去分詞
- **glad** 形 ①うれしい, 喜ばしい ②《be ~ to ~》~してうれしい, 喜んで~する
- **glass** 名 ガラス (状のもの), コップ, グラス

- **go** 動①行く, 出かける ②動く ③進む, 経過する, いたる ④(ある状態に)なる **be going to** ～するつもりである **go across** 横断する, 渡る **go ahead** (仕事を)続ける **go back to** ～に帰る[戻る] **go down** 下に降りる **go for** ～に出かける, ～を追い求める **go into** ～に入る **go off toward** ～に向かう **go on** 続く, 続ける, 進み続ける, 起こる, 発生する **go on living** 生きていく **go out** 外出する, 外へ出る **go through** 通り抜ける **go to bed** 床につく, 寝る **go up and down** 上がり下がりする **go with** ～と一緒に行く, ～と調和する **let it go** あきらめる, 手を離す
- **gold** 名 金, 金貨, 金製品, 金色 形 金の, 金製の, 金色の
- **gone** 動 go(行く)の過去分詞 形 去った, 使い果たした, 死んだ
- **good** 形 ①よい, 上手な, 優れた, 美しい ②(数量・程度が)かなりの, 相当な
- **got** 動 get(得る)の過去, 過去分詞
- **gotten** 動 get(得る)の過去分詞
- **gourd** 名 ウリ類《植物》**snake gourd** カラスウリ
- **grab** 動 ふいにつかむ
- **grass** 名 草, 牧草(地), 芝生
- **great** 形 ①大きい, 広大な, (量や程度が)たいへんな ②偉大な, 優れた ③すばらしい, おもしろい
- **grew** 動 grow(成長する)の過去
- **ground** 名 地面, 土, 土地 **fall to the ground** 転ぶ **on the ground** 地面に
- **grow** 動 ①成長する, 育つ, 育てる ②増大する, 大きくなる, (次第に～に)なる **grow tired** 飽きがくる **the air grow close** 空気がもやがかる, 薄闇が立ち込める
- **grown** 動 grow(成長する)の過去分詞

H

- **Haaa** 間 悪魔の叫んだ声
- **had** 動 have(持つ)の過去, 過去分詞 助 haveの過去《過去完了の文をつくる》
- **Hades** 名 ①《ギリシア神話》ハデス ②地獄《俗》**King of Hades** 閻魔大王
- **half** 名 半分
- **hand** 名 手 **take someone by the hand** (人の)手を取る[引く] 動 手渡す
- **hang** 動 かかる, かける, つるす, ぶら下がる **hang down** ぶら下がる
- **happen** 動 ①(出来事が)起こる, 生じる ②偶然[たまたま]～する **happen to** たまたま～する, 偶然～する
- **happy** 形 幸せな, うれしい, 幸運な, 満足して
- **hard** 形 ①堅い ②激しい, むずかしい ③熱心な, 勤勉な ④無情な, 耐えがたい, 厳しい, きつい **hard to** ～し難い 副 ①一生懸命に ②激しく ③堅く
- **has** 動 have(持つ)の3人称単数現在 助 haveの3人称単数現在《現在完了の文をつくる》
- **hat** 名 (縁のある)帽子
- **hate** 動 嫌う, 憎む, (～するのを)いやがる
- **have** 動 ①持つ, 持っている, 抱く ②(～が)ある, いる ③食べる, 飲む ④経験する, (病気に)かかる ⑤催す, 開く ⑥(人に)～させる **have no idea** わからない **have one's way with** ～を思い通りにする **have someone do** (人に)～させる **have to** ～しなければならない 助《《have+過去分詞》の形で現在完了の文をつくる》～した, ～したことがある, ずっと～している **could have done** ～だったかもしれない《仮定法》**have been to** ～へ行ったことがある
- **he** 代 彼は[が]

Word List

- □ **head** 名 頭
- □ **hear** 動 聞く, 聞こえる
- □ **heard** 動 hear（聞く）の過去, 過去分詞
- □ **heart** 名 ①心臓, 胸 ②心, 感情, ハート
- □ **heavy** 形 重い, 激しい, つらい
- □ **held** 動 hold（つかむ）の過去, 過去分詞
- □ **hello** 間 ①こんにちは, やあ ②《電話で》もしもし
- □ **help** 動 ①助ける, 手伝う ②給仕する **cannot help ~ing** ~せずにはいられない 名 助け, 手伝い
- □ **her** 代 ①彼女を［に］ ②彼女の
- □ **here** 副 ①ここに［で］ ②《- is [are] ~》ここに~がある ③さあ, そら **here and there** あちこちで 名 ここ
- □ **hidden** 形 隠れた, 秘密の
- □ **high** 形 ①高い ②気高い, 高価な 副 ①高く ②ぜいたくに
- □ **hill** 名 丘, 塚
- □ **him** 代 彼を［に］
- □ **himself** 代 彼自身
- □ **his** 代 ①彼の ②彼のもの
- □ **history** 名 歴史, 経歴
- □ **hit** 動 ①打つ, なぐる ②ぶつける, ぶつかる 名 打撃
- □ **hold** 動 ①つかむ, 持つ, 抱く ②保つ, 持ちこたえる ③収納できる, 入れることができる ④（会などを）開く **hold on** しっかりつかまる **hold on to** ~にしがみつく, ~をつかんで放さない **hold up** ①維持する, 支える ②~を持ち上げる 名 ①つかむこと, 保有 ②支配［理解］力 **take hold of** ~をつかむ, 捕らえる, 制する
- □ **hole** 名 ①穴, すき間 ②苦境, 困難 **Road of the Dark Hole** 闇穴道, この世と地獄とを結ぶ道
- □ **home** 名 家, 自国, 故郷, 家庭
- □ **hope** 動 望む, (~であるようにと)思う
- □ **horse** 名 馬
- □ **horse fly** アブ
- □ **hot** 形 暑い, 熱い
- □ **hour** 名 1時間, 時間
- □ **house** 名 ①家, 家庭 ②（特定の目的のための）建物, 小屋 **bath house** 浴場
- □ **how** 副 ①どうやって, どれくらい, どんなふうに ②なんて（~だろう）③《関係副詞》~する方法 **how to** ~する方法 **no matter how** どんなに~であろうとも
- □ **human** 名 人間 **human being** 人, 人間
- □ **hung** 動 hang（かかる）の過去, 過去分詞
- □ **hungry** 形 空腹の, 飢えた
- □ **hunter** 名 ①狩りをする人, 狩人, ハンター ②猟馬, 猟犬 **bounty hunter** 賞金稼ぎ
- □ **hurt** 動 傷つける, 痛む, 害する
- □ **husband** 名 夫

I

- □ **I** 代 私は［が］
- □ **ice** 名 氷
- □ **idea** 名 考え, 意見, アイデア, 計画 **have no idea** わからない
- □ **if** 接 もし~ならば, たとえ~でも, ~かどうか **If +《主語》+ could** ~できればなあ《仮定法》**as if** あたかも~のように, まるで~みたいに **even if** たとえ~でも **see if** ~かどうかを確かめる
- □ **Ike-no-o (Town)** 池の尾《町名》
- □ **image** 名 ①印象, 姿 ②画像, 映像
- □ **important** 形 重要な, 大切な, 有力な
- □ **impossible** 形 不可能な, できない, あり［起こり］えない
- □ **in** 前 ①《場所・位置・所属》~（の中）に［で・の］ ②《時》~（の時）に［の・で］,

～後(に), ～の間(に) ③《方法・手段》～で ④～を身につけて, ～を着て ⑤～に関して, ～について ⑥《状態》～の状態で **in a way** ある意味では **in any case** とにかく **in case** ～だといけないので, 念のため, 万が一 **in fact** つまり, 実は, 要するに **in front of** ～の前に, ～の正面に **in one place** 一ヶ所に 副中へ[に], 内へ[に]

- **increase** 動増加[増強]する, 増やす, 増える
- **instead** 副その代わりに
- **interest** 名①興味, 関心 ②利害(関係), 利益 ③利子, 利息
- **interested** 形興味を持った, 関心のある
- **into** 前①《動作・運動の方向》～の中へ[に] ②《変化》～に[へ] **fall into** ～に陥る, ～してしまう **get into** ～に入る, 入り込む **go into** ～に入る **lead into** (ある場所)へ導く **look into** ①～を検討する, ～を研究する ②～の中を見る, ～をのぞき込む **put ～ into ～** ～を…の状態にする, ～を…に突っ込む
- **is** 動 be (～である)の3人称単数現在
- **it** 代①それは[が], それを[に] ②《天候・日時・距離・寒暖などを示す》 **It is ～ for someone to …** …するのは～だ **That's it.** それだけのことだ。
- **itch** 動①かゆい, むずむずする ②ほしくてたまらない, したくてたまらない
- **itchy** 形かゆい, むずむずする
- **its** 代それの, あれの

J

- **Japan** 名日本《国名》
- **jaw** 名①あご ②《-s》あご状のもの
- **just** 副①まさに, ちょうど, (～し

た)ばかり ②ほんの, 単に, ただ～だけ ③ちょっと **do just that** その通りにやる **just as** (ちょうど)であろうとおり **just for a second** ほんの一瞬 **just like that** 簡単に, あっという間に **just then** そのとたんに

K

- **Kanazawa Takehiro** 金沢武弘《人名。死んでいた男性》
- **keep** 動①とっておく, 保つ, 続ける ②(～を…に)しておく ③飼う, 養う ④経営する ⑤守る **keep away from** ～に近寄らない **keep someone from** ～から(人)を阻む
- **kept** keep (とっておく)の過去, 過去分詞
- **kick** 動ける, キックする
- **kill** 動殺す, 消す, 枯らす
- **kind** 形親切な, 優しい **be kind to** ～に親切である 名種類 **in a kind of way** 多少, いくぶん **kind of** ある程度, いくらか, ～のようなもの[人]
- **king** 名王, 国王
- **King of Hades** 閻魔大王
- **Kiyomizu Temple** 清水寺
- **knew** 動 know (知っている)の過去
- **know** 動①知っている, 知る, (～が)わかる, 理解している ②知り合いである **before you [I] know it** あっという間に, 驚くほど早く
- **known** 動 know (知っている)の過去分詞 形知られた **be known as** ～として知られている
- **Kyoto** 名京都《地名》

L

- **lake** 名湖, 湖水, 池
- **large** 形大きい
- **last** 形①《the -》最後の ②この前

Word List

- **laugh** 動笑う laugh at ~を見て[聞いて]笑う 名笑い(声)
- **lead** 動①導く, 案内する ②(生活を)送る lead a life 生活を送る, 暮らす lead into (ある場所)へ導く
- **leaf** 名葉
- **leap** 動①跳ぶ ②跳び越える
- **learn** 動学ぶ, 習う, 教わる, 知識[経験]を得る
- **leave** 動①出発する, 去る ②残す, 置き忘れる ③(~を…の)ままにしておく ④ゆだねる leave behind あとにする, ~を置き去りにする leave for ~に向かって出発する leave the matter to ~にその件をまかせる
- **leaves** 名 leaf (葉)の複数
- **led** 動 lead (導く)の過去, 過去分詞
- **left** 動 leave (去る, ~をあとに残す)の過去, 過去分詞
- **less** 副 ~より少なく, ~ほどでなく
- **let** 動(人に~)させる, (~するのを)許す, (~をある状態に)する let it go あきらめる, 手を離す let out (声を)出す, 発する
- **life** 名①生命, 生物 ②一生, 生涯, 人生 ③生活, 暮らし, 世の中 lead a life 生活を送る, 暮らす
- **lift** 動持ち上げる, 上がる
- **light** 名光, 明かり 形①明るい ②(色が)薄い, 淡い ③軽い, 容易な
- **light-blue** 形ライトブルーの, 淡い青色の
- **like** 動好む, 好きである would like to ~したいと思う 前~に似ている, ~のような just like that 簡単に, あっという間に like a man 男らしく look like ~のように見える, ~に似ている sound like ~のように聞こえる
- **lip** 名唇, 《-s》口
- **listen** 動《-to~》~を聞く, ~に耳を傾ける
- **little** 形①小さい, 幼い ②少しの, 短い ③ほとんど~ない, 《a-》少しはある
- **live** 動住む, 暮らす, 生きている go on living 生きていく live with ~耐える, 我慢する
- **long** 形①長い, 長期の ②《長さ・距離・時間などを示す語句を伴って》~の長さ[距離・時間]の as long as ~する以上は, ~である限りは for long 長い間 no longer もはや~でない[~しない] 名長い期間 before long やがて, まもなく
- **look** 動①見る ②(~に)見える, (~の)顔つきをする ③注意する ④《間投詞のように》ほら, ねえ look around まわりを見回す look away ~の方を見る look back at ~に視線を戻す, ~を振り返って見る look down 見下ろす look down at ~に目[視線]を落とす look down on ~を見下す look for ~を探す look into ①~を検討する, ~を研究する ②~の中を見る, ~をのぞき込む look like ~のように見える, ~に似ている look up 見上げる, 調べる look straight ahead まっすぐ前を見る
- **lose** 動①失う, 迷う, 忘れる ②負ける, 失敗する lose oneself in thought 物思いにふける
- **lost** 動 lose (失う)の過去, 過去分詞
- **lot** 名たくさん, たいへん, 《a - of ~ / -s of ~》たくさんの~
- **loud** 形大声の, 騒がしい 副大声に[で] out loud 大きな声で
- **low** 形①低い, 弱い ②低級の, 劣等な
- **luck** 名運, 幸運, めぐり合わせ bad luck 災難, 不運, 悪運
- **lucky** 形幸運な, 運のよい, 縁起のよい
- **Luoyang** 名洛陽《地名。現在の中国河南省河南》
- **luxury** 名豪華さ, 贅沢(品)

Short Stories of Ryunosuke Akutagawa

M

- **made** 動 make（作る）の過去, 過去分詞
- **make** 動 ①作る, 得る ②行う,（～に）なる ③（～を…に）する,（～を…）させる **make all the difference** 状況を一変させる **make one's way through** ～の間を進む, ～を通り抜ける **make use of** ～を利用する, ～を生かす
- **man** 名 男性, 人, 人類 **like a man** 男らしく
- **many** 形 多数の, たくさんの **so many** 非常に多くの
- **Masago** 名 真砂《人名。死んでいた男性の妻》
- **matter** 名 物, 事, 事件, 問題 **leave the matter to** ～にその件をまかせる **no matter** ～を問わず, どうでもいい **no matter how** どんなに～であろうとも
- **may** 助 ①～かもしれない ②～してもよい, ～できる
- **maybe** 副 たぶん, おそらく
- **me** 代 私を[に]
- **mean** 動 ①意味する ②（～のつもりで）言う, 意図する ③～するつもりである
- **meant** 動 mean（意味する）の過去, 過去分詞
- **medicine** 名 薬
- **medium** 名 霊媒師, 霊能者
- **men** 名 man（男性）の複数
- **met** 動 meet（会う）の過去, 過去分詞
- **meter** 名 ①メートル《長さの単位》②計量器, 計量する人
- **middle** 名 中間, 最中
- **might** 助《mayの過去》①～かもしれない ②～してもよい, ～できる
- **millimeter** 名 ミリメートル《長さの単位》
- **minute** 名 ①（時間の）分 ②ちょっとの間
- **mirror** 名 鏡
- **mistake** 名 誤り, 誤解, 間違い
- **moan** 動 うめき声を出す
- **moment** 名 ①瞬間, ちょっとの間 ②（特定の）時, 時期
- **money** 名 金, 通貨
- **monk** 名 修道士, 僧
- **moon** 名 月, 月光
- **more** 形 ①もっと多くの ②それ以上の, 余分の 副 もっと, さらに多く, いっそう **more than** ～以上 **no more** もう～ない **not any more** もはや～しない **once more** もう一度 **the more ～ the more …** ～すればするほどますます… 名 もっと多くの物[人]
- **morning** 名 朝, 午前
- **most** 形 ①最も多い ②たいていの, 大部分の 代 ①大部分, ほとんど ②最多数, 最大限
- **mother** 名 母, 母親
- **mountain** 名 ①山 ②《the ～ M-s》～山脈
- **mouth** 名 ①口 ②言葉, 発言
- **move** 動 動く, 動かす 名 動き, 運動
- **Mr.** 名《男性に対して》～さん, ～氏, ～先生
- **Mt.** 名 ～山（=mount）
- **much** 形（量・程度が）多くの, 多量の **too much** 過度の 副 ①とても, たいへん ②《比較級・最上級を修飾して》ずっと, はるかに
- **must** 助 ①～しなければならない ②～に違いない
- **my** 代 私の
- **myself** 代 私自身

N

- **name** 名 名前
- **near** 前 ～の近くに, ～のそばに 副

Word List

近くに, 親密で **get near** 接近する
- **need** 名 ①必要(性), 《-s》必要なもの ②まさかの時
- **never** 副 決して[少しも]～ない, 一度も[二度と]～ない **never ever** 絶対に, 決して
- **Never Ending Place** 森羅殿, 閻魔大王の宮殿
- **new** 形 ①新しい, 新規の ②新鮮な, できたての
- **next** 形 ①次の, 翌～ ②隣の 副 ①次に ②隣に **next to** ～のとなりに, ～の次に
- **night** 名 夜, 晩 **day and night** 昼も夜も
- **nine** 名 9(の数字), 9人[個] 形 9の, 9人[個]の
- **nineteen** 名 19(の数字), 19人[個] 形 19の, 19人[個]の
- **no** 副 ①いいえ, いや ②少しも～ない 形 ①～がない, 少しも～ない, ～どころでない, ～禁止 **have no idea** わからない **no longer** もはや～でない[～しない] **no matter** ～を問わず, どうでもいい **no matter how** どんなに～であろうとも **no more** もう～ない **no one** 誰も[一人も]～ない **no sooner** ～するや否や
- **no one** 誰も[一人も]～ない
- **nod** 動 うなずく
- **noon** 名 ①正午, 真昼 ②《the –》全盛期
- **north** 名《the –》北, 北部
- **nose** 名 鼻, 嗅覚, におい
- **not** 副 ～でない, ～しない **not any more** もはや～しない **not ～ at all** 少しも[全然]～ない **not ～ but …** ～ではなくて… **whether or not** かどうか
- **nothing** 代 何も～ない[しない] **nothing but** ただ～だけ, ～にすぎない, ～のほかは何も…ない
- **now** 副 ①今(では), 現在 ②今すぐに ③では, さて **now that** 今や～だから, ～からには **right now** 今

すぐに, たった今 名 今, 現在 **from now on** 今後
- **nowhere** 副 どこにも～ない
- **number** 名 ①数, 数字, 番号 ②～号, ～番 ③《-s》多数 **a number of** いくつかの～, 多くの～

O

- **o'clock** 副 ～時
- **of** 前 ①《所有・所属・部分》～の, ～に属する ②《性質・特徴・材料》～の, ～製の ③《部分》～のうち ④《分離・除去》～から **of course** もちろん, 当然 **of one's own** 自分自身の
- **off** 副 ①離れて ②はずれて ③止まって ④休んで **fly off** 飛び去る **set off** 出発する, 発射する **take off** (衣服を)脱ぐ, 取り去る, ～を取り除く 形 ①離れて ②季節はずれの ③休みの **be off to** ～へ出かける 前 ～を離れて, ～をはずれて, (値段が)～引きの
- **often** 副 しばしば, たびたび
- **oh** 間 ああ, おや, まあ
- **oil** 名 油
- **oily** 形 油の, 油っこい, 油で汚れた **oily bump** 角栓, 皮脂の固まり
- **old** 形 ①年取った, 老いた ②～歳の ③古い, 昔の
- **on** 前 ①《場所・接触》～(の上)に ②《日・時》～に, ～と同時に, ～のすぐ後で ③《関係・従事》～に関して, ～について, ～して **on business** 仕事で **on one's back** あおむけに **on one's way** 途中で 副 ①身につけて, 上に ②前へ, 続けて
- **once** 副 ①一度, 1回 ②かつて **once in a while** たまに, 時々 **once more** もう一度 名 一度, 1回 **all at once** 突然, 出し抜けに **at once** すぐに, 同時に 接 いったん～すると
- **one** 名 1(の数字), 1人[個] **as ～ as one can** できる限り～ **no one** 誰も[一人も]～ない **one after**

another 次々に, 1つ[人]ずつ **one another** お互い **one of ~** の1つ[人] 形 ①1の, 1人[個]の ②ある~ ③《the –》唯一の **one day**《過去の》ある日,《未来の》いつか 代 ①《一般の》人, ある物 ②一方, 片方 ③~なもの

- **oneself** 熟 **by oneself** 一人で, 自分だけで, 独力で **for oneself** 独力で, 自分のために **say to oneself** ひとり言を言う, 心に思う
- **only** 形 唯一の **one and only** 唯一無二の 副 ①単に, ~にすぎない, ただ~だけ ②やっと
- **onto** 前 ~の上へ[に]
- **open** 形 ①開いた, 広々とした ②公開された 動 ①開く, 始まる ②広がる, 広げる ③打ち明ける
- **or** 接 ①~か…, または ②さもないと ③すなわち, 言い換えると
- **order** 名 ①順序 ②整理, 整頓 ③命令, 注文(品) 動 ①(~するよう)命じる, 注文する ②整頓する, 整理する
- **other** 形 ①ほかの, 異なった ②(2つのうち)もう一方の, (3つ以上のうち)残りの 代 ①ほかの人[物] ②《the –》残りの人 **each other** お互いに
- **out** 副 ①外へ[に], 不在で, 離れて ②世に出て ③消えて ④すっかり **out of ~** から外へ, ~から抜け出し **out of step with** ~と調和しないで 前 ~から外へ[に]
- **outside** 副 外へ, 外側に 前 ~の外に[で・の・へ], ~の範囲を越えて
- **over** 前 ①~の上の[に], ~を一面に覆って ②~を越えて, ~以上に, ~よりまさって ③~の向こう側の[に] ④~の間 副 ①上に, 一面に, ずっと **over and over** 何度も繰り返して 形 ①上部の, 上位の, 過多の ②終わって, すんで **be over** 終わる
- **own** 形 自身の **of one's own** 自分自身の

P

- **pain** 名 ①痛み, 苦悩 ②《-s》骨折り, 苦労 動 苦痛を与える, 痛む
- **palomino** 名 パロミノ種の馬, 月毛《薄い黄金色の毛色を持つ馬種》
- **part** 名 部分, 割合
- **party** 名 パーティー, 会, 集まり
- **pass** 動 ①過ぎる, 通る ②(年月が)たつ
- **path** 名 (踏まれてできた)小道, 歩道
- **peach** 名 モモ(桃)
- **people** 名 (一般に)人々, 民衆
- **perfect** 形 完璧な, 完全な
- **person** 名 ①人 ②人格, 人柄
- **pick** 動 ①(花・果実などを)摘む, もぐ ②選ぶ, 精選する ③つつく, ついて穴をあける, ほじくり出す ④(~を)摘み取る **pick up** 拾い上げる
- **picture** 名 絵, 写真
- **piece** 名 ①一片, 部分 ②1個, 1本
- **pine** 名 マツ(松), マツ材
- **place** 名 ①場所, 建物 ②余地, 空間 ③《one's –》家, 部屋 **in one place** 一ヶ所に **in the first place** 最初に **Never Ending Place** 森羅殿, 閻魔大王の宮殿 **take place** 行われる, 起こる
- **plan** 動 計画する
- **play** 動 遊ぶ
- **please** 動 喜ばす, 満足させる 間 どうぞ, お願いします
- **pleased** 形 喜んだ, 気に入った
- **point** 名 ①先, 先端 ②点 ③地点, 時点, 箇所 ④《the –》要点 **at this point** 現在のところ 動 ①(~を)指す, 向ける ②とがらせる **point out** 指し示す, 指摘する, 目を向ける, 目を向けさせる
- **pond** 名 池
- **poor** 形 ①貧しい, 乏しい, 粗末な, 貧弱な ②劣った, へたな ③不幸な, 哀れな, 気の毒な

Word List

- **pound** 動 どんどんたたく
- **prepare** 動 ①準備[用意]をする ②覚悟する[させる]
- **prepared** 形 準備[用意]のできた
- **pretty** 形 ①かわいい, きれいな ②相当な
- **priest** 名 聖職者, 牧師, 僧侶
- **problem** 名 問題, 難問
- **promise** 名 約束
- **pull** 動 ①引く, 引っ張る ②引きつける **pull out** 引き抜く, 引き出す, 取り出す
- **push** 動 ①押す, 押し進める, 押し進める ②進む, 突き出る **push down into** ～を…に突き落とす
- **put** 動 ①置く, のせる ②入れる, つける ③(ある状態に)する ④putの過去, 過去分詞 **put away** 片づける, 取っておく **put in** ～の中に入れる **put up** 戦って抵抗する **put ～ into …** ～を…の状態にする, ～を…に突っ込む **put through** ～を経験させる

Q

- **question** 名 質問, 疑問, 問題
- **quick** 形 (動作が)速い, すばやい
- **quickly** 副 敏速に, 急いで
- **quiet** 形 ①静かな, 穏やかな, じっとした ②おとなしい, 無口な, 目立たない
- **quietly** 副 ①静かに ②平穏に, 控えめに
- **quite** 副 ①まったく, すっかり, 完全に ②かなり, ずいぶん ③ほとんど

R

- **rain** 名 雨, 降雨 動 雨が降る
- **raise** 動 ①上げる, 高める ②起こす
- **ran** 動 run (走る)の過去
- **reach** 動 着く, 到着する, 届く
- **read** 動 読む, 読書する **read out** 声を出して読む, 読み上げる
- **ready** 形 用意[準備]ができた, まさに～しようとする, 今にも～せんばかりの **be ready to** すぐに[いつでも]～できる, ～する構えで **get ready** 用意[支度]をする
- **real** 形 実際の, 実在する, 本物の
- **really** 副 用意[準備]する
- **reason** 名 ①理由 ②理性, 道理 **reason for** ～の理由
- **red** 形 赤い 名 赤, 赤色
- **remember** 動 思い出す, 覚えている, 忘れないでいる
- **reply** 動 答える, 返事をする, 応答する
- **rest** 動 ①休む, 眠る ②休止する, 静止する ③(～に)基づいている ④(～の)ままである **rest on** ～の上に載っている
- **return** 動 帰る, 戻る, 返す **return to** ～に戻る, ～に帰る
- **rice** 名 米, 飯
- **rich** 形 ①富んだ, 金持ちの ②豊かな, 濃い, 深い
- **ride** 動 乗る, 乗って行く, 馬に乗る
- **right** 形 ①正しい ②適切な **all right** 大丈夫で, よろしい, 申し分ない, わかった, 承知した 副 ①すぐに, すぐに ②ちょうど, 正確に **right away** すぐに **right now** 今すぐに, たった今
- **rise** 動 上がる, 昇る **rise up** わき起こる
- **river** 名 川
- **road** 名 ①道路, 道, 通り ②手段, 方法
- **Road of the Dark Hole** 闇穴道, この世と地獄とを結ぶ道
- **robber** 名 泥棒, 強盗
- **rock** 名 岩, 岸壁, 岩石
- **room** 名 部屋

- **rope** 名 綱, なわ, ロープ
- **rose** 動 rise (昇る) の過去
- **round** 形 丸い, 円形の
- **run** 動 走る **run after** ～を追いかける

S

- **sad** 形 ①悲しい, 悲しげな ②惨めな, 不運な
- **sadly** 副 悲しそうに, 不幸にも
- **said** 動 say (言う) の過去, 過去分詞
- **same** 形 ①同じ, 同様の ②前述の **all the same** とにかく, いずれにせよ **the same ～ as** …と同じ (ような) **the same way as** ～と同じように 代《the -》同一の人[物]副《the -》同様に
- **samurai** 名 侍
- **sang** 動 sing (歌う) の過去
- **sat** 動 sit (座る) の過去, 過去分詞
- **sausage** 名 ソーセージ
- **saw** 動 see (見る) の過去
- **say** 動 言う, 口に出す **say to oneself** ひとり言を言う, 心に思う **strange to say** 不思議な話だが
- **scene** 名 ①光景, 風景 ②(劇の) 場, 一幕 ③(事件の) 現場
- **sea** 名 海, 《the ～ S-, the S- of ～》～海
- **second** 名 ①第2 (の人[物]) ②(時間の) 秒, 瞬時 **just for a second** ほんの一瞬 形 第2の, 2番の 副 第2に
- **see** 動 ①見る, 見える, 見物する ②(～と) わかる, 認識する, 経験する ③会う ④考える, 確かめる, 調べる ⑤気をつける **see if** ～かどうかを確かめる **see ～ as** …～を…と考える **you see** あのね, いいですか
- **seem** 動 (～に) 見える, (～のように) 思われる
- **seen** 動 see (見る) の過去分詞

- **Seiobo** 名 西王母《人名》
- **Sekiyama** 名 関山《別名, 逢坂山》
- **sell** 動 売る, 売っている, 売れる
- **set** 動 ①置く, 当てる, つける ②整える, 設定する ③(太陽・月などが) 沈む ④(～を…の状態に) する, させる ⑤set の過去, 過去分詞 **set off** 出発する 名 一そろい, セット
- **setting** 名 設定, 周囲の環境
- **seven** 名 7(の数字), 7人[個] 形 7の, 7人[個] の
- **shadow** 名 影, 暗がり
- **shame** 名 ①恥, 恥辱 ②恥ずべきこと, ひどいこと 動 恥をかかせる, 侮辱する
- **shape** 名 形, 姿, 型
- **she** 代 彼女は[が]
- **shocked** 形 ～にショックを受けて, 憤慨して
- **short** 形 ①短い ②背の低い ③不足している
- **should** 助 ～すべきである, ～したほうがよい
- **shout** 動 叫ぶ, 大声で言う, どなりつける
- **show** 動 ①見せる, 示す, 見える ②明らかにする, 教える
- **sick** 形 ①病気の ②むかついて, いや気がさして **feel sick** 気分が悪い
- **side** 名 側, 横, そば, 斜面
- **sigh** 動 ため息をつく, ため息をついて言う
- **sign** 名 ①きざし, 徴候 ②跡 ③看板
- **simple** 形 ①単純な, 簡単な, 質素な ②単一の, 単独の ③普通の, ただの
- **simply** 副 ①簡単に ②単に, ただ
- **since** 接 ①～以来 ②～だから 前 ～以来 副 それ以来 **ever since** それ以来ずっと
- **sing** 動 ①(歌を) 歌う ②さえずる **sing of** ～のことを歌う

Word List

- □ **singing** 名歌うこと, 歌声
- □ **single** 形たった1つの
- □ **sit** 動①座る, 腰掛ける ②止まる ③位置する **sit across** 〜の向かいに座る **sit on** 〜の上に乗る, 〜の上に乗って動けないようにする
- □ **six** 名6(の数字), 6人[個] 形6の, 6人[個]の
- □ **sixty** 名60(の数字), 60人[個] 形60の, 60人[個]の
- □ **size** 名大きさ, 寸法, サイズ
- □ **skin** 名皮膚
- □ **sky** 名空, 天空, 大空
- □ **sleep** 動眠る, 寝る
- □ **sleeve** 名袖, たもと, スリーブ
- □ **slept** 動 sleep(眠る)の過去, 過去分詞
- □ **small** 形小さい, 少ない
- □ **smile** 動微笑する, にっこり笑う **smile at** 〜に微笑みかける 名微笑, ほほえみ
- □ **snake** 名ヘビ(蛇)
- □ **snake gourd** カラスウリ
- □ **sneeze** 動くしゃみをする
- □ **so** 副①とても ②同様に, 〜もまた ③《先行する句・節の代用》そのように, そう **and so** そこで, それだから, それで **so many** 非常に多くの **so that** 〜するために, それで, 〜できるように **so 〜 that …** 非常に〜なので… 接①だから, それで ②では, さて
- □ **Sogo, Mt.** 蒼梧山
- □ **some** 形①いくつかの, 多少の ②ある, 誰か, 何か
- □ **someone** 代ある人, 誰か
- □ **something** 代①ある物, 何か ②いくぶん, 多少
- □ **son** 名息子, 子弟, 〜の子
- □ **song** 名歌, 詩歌, 鳴き声
- □ **soon** 副まもなく, すぐに, すみやかに **as soon as** 〜するとすぐ, 〜するや否や **no sooner** 〜するや否や
- □ **sorry** 形気の毒に[申し訳なく]思う, 残念な **feel sorry for** 〜をかわいそうに思う
- □ **sound** 名音, 騒音, 響き, サウンド
- □ **south** 名《the -》南, 南方, 南部
- □ **space** 名①空間, 宇宙 ②すき間, 余地, 場所, 間
- □ **speak** 動話す, 言う, 演説する **speak to** 〜と話す
- □ **spear** 名槍, 投げ槍
- □ **special** 形①特別の, 特殊の, 臨時の ②専門の
- □ **spend** 動①(金などを)使う, 消費[浪費]する ②(時を)過ごす
- □ **spent** 動 spend(使う)の過去, 過去分詞
- □ **spirit** 名①霊 ②精神, 気力 **evil spirit** 魔性
- □ **spoke** 動 speak(話す)の過去
- □ **spoken** 動 speak(話す)の過去分詞
- □ **spread** 動広がる, 広げる, 伸びる, 伸ばす
- □ **spring** 名春
- □ **stab** 動(突き)刺す
- □ **stand** 動立つ, 立たせる, 立っている, ある **stand by** そばに立つ, 傍観する, 待機する **stand out** 突き出る, 目立つ
- □ **star** 名星, 星形の物
- □ **start** 動出発する, 始まる, 始める
- □ **statue** 名像
- □ **stay** 動①とどまる, 泊まる, 滞在する ②持続する, (〜の)ままでいる **stay on** 居残る, とどまる, (電灯などが)ついたままである
- □ **step** 名①歩み, 1歩(の距離) ②段階 ③踏み段, 階段 **out of step with** 〜と調和しない 動歩む, 踏んで **step on** 〜を踏みつける
- □ **stick** 名棒, 杖
- □ **still** 副①まだ, 今でも ②それでも(なお)

121

Short Stories of Ryunosuke Akutagawa

- **stomach** 名 ①胃, 腹 ②食欲, 欲望, 好み
- **stood** 動 stand (立つ) の過去, 過去分詞
- **stop** 動 ①やめる, やめさせる, 止める, 止まる ②立ち止まる **stop by** 途中で立ち寄る, ちょっと訪ねる **stop doing** ~するのをやめる
- **story** 名 物語, 話
- **straight** 形 ①一直線の, まっすぐな, 直立[垂直]の ②率直な, 整然とした 副 ①一直線に, まっすぐに, 垂直に ②率直に
- **strange** 形 ①知らない, 見[聞]き慣れない ②奇妙な, 変わった **strange to say** 不思議な話だが
- **street** 名 ①街路 ②《S-》~通り
- **strike** 動 打つ, ぶつかる
- **strong** 形 強い, 堅固な, 強烈な
- **struck** 動 strike (打つ) の過去, 過去分詞
- **subject** 名 話題, 議題, 主題
- **such** 形 ①そのような, このような ②そんなに, とても, 非常に **such a** そのような **such as** たとえば~, ~のような
- **suddenly** 副 突然, 急に
- **suffer** 動 ①(苦痛・損害などを)受ける, こうむる ②(病気に)なる, 苦しむ, 悩む
- **suikan clothes** 水干《平安・鎌倉時代の男性の普段着》
- **sun** 名 《the -》太陽, 日
- **sure** 形 確かな, 確実な
- **surprise** 名 驚き, 不意打ち **catch someone by surprise** 不意打ちをかける, 不意をつく
- **surprised** 形 驚いた
- **surprising** 形 驚くべき, 意外な
- **sutra** 名 スートラ, 経典
- **sweet** 形 ①甘い ②快い
- **sword** 名 剣, 刀

T

- **table** 名 テーブル, 食卓, 台
- **Taizan, Mt.** 泰山
- **Tajomaru** 多襄丸《人名。盗賊》
- **take** 動 ①取る, 持つ ②持って[連れて]いく, 捕らえる ③乗る ④(時間・労力を)費やす, 必要とする ⑤(ある動作を)する ⑥飲む ⑦耐える, 受け入れる **take care of** ~の世話をする, ~面倒を見る, ~を管理する **take hold of** ~をつかむ, 捕らえる, 制する **take off** (衣服を)脱ぐ, 取り去る, ~を外す **take on** (人を)弟子としてとる **take out** 取り出す **take out of** ~から出す, ~に連れ出す **take place** 行われる, 起こる **take someone by the hand** (人の)手を取る[引く]
- **Takehiro, Kanazawa** 金沢武弘《人名。死んでいた男性》
- **taken** 動 take (取る) の過去分詞
- **talk** 動 話す, 語る, 相談する
- **tall** 形 高い, 背の高い
- **Tang** 名 唐《中国の王朝》
- **taste** 名 味, 風味
- **taught** 動 teach (教える) の過去, 過去分詞
- **tea** 名 茶, 紅茶
- **teach** 動 教える
- **tear** 名 涙
- **Tekkanshi** 鉄冠子《人名》
- **tell** 動 ①話す, 言う, 語る ②教える, 知らせる, 伝える ③わかる, 見分ける **tell ~ to …** ~に…するように言う
- **temple** 名 寺
- **tempt** 動 誘う, 誘惑する, 導く, 心を引きつける
- **terrible** 形 恐ろしい, ひどい, ものすごい, つらい
- **than** 接 ~よりも, ~以上に **more than** ~以上
- **thank** 動 感謝する, 礼を言う

Word List

thank ~ for ~に対して礼を言う

- **that** 形 その,あの this and that あちこちへ 代 ①それ,あれ,その[あの]人[物] ②《関係代名詞》~である… after that その後 That's it. それだけのことだ。 That's too bad. 残念だ。 接 ~ということ,~なので,~だから now that 今や~だから,~からには so that ~するために,それで,~できるように so ~ that … 非常に~なので…
- **the** 冠 ①その,あの ②《形容詞の前で》~な人々 副《- +比較級,- +比較級》~すればするほど.
- **their** 代 彼(女)らの,それらの
- **them** 代 彼(女)らを[に],それらを[に] both of them 彼ら[それら]両方とも
- **then** 副 その時(に・は),それから,次に just then そのとたんに
- **there** 副 ①そこに[で・の],そこへ,あそこへ ②《- is [are]》~がある[いる] here and there あちこちで
- **these** 形 これらの,この
- **they** 代 ①彼(女)らは[が],それらは[が] ②(一般の)人々は[が]
- **thing** 名 ①物,事 ②《-s》事情,事柄 ③《one's -s》持ち物,身の回り品 ④人,やつ
- **think** 動 思う,考える think of ~ のことを考える,~を思いつく,考え出す to think that《驚きや悲しみをこめて》~だとはねえ
- **third** 名 第3(の人[物]) 形 第3の,3番の
- **this** 形 ①この,こちらの,これを ②今の,現在の at this point 現在のところ this way and that あちこちへ 代 ①これ,この人[物] ②今,ここ this and that あれやこれや
- **those** 形 それらの,あれらの 代 それら[あれら]の人[物]
- **though** 副 しかし
- **thought** 動 think(思う)の過去,過去分詞 名 考え,意見 lose oneself in thought 物思いにふける

- **thousand** 名 ①1000(の数字),1000人[個] ②《-s》何千,多数 形 ①1000の,1000人[個]の ②多数の
- **three** 名 3(の数字),3人[個] 形 3の,3人[個]の
- **threw** 動 throw(投げる)の過去
- **through** 前 ~を通して,~中を[に],~中 come through 通り抜ける,成功する,期待に沿う cut through 切り開く go through 通り抜ける make one's way through ~の間を進む,~を通り抜ける
- **throw** 動 投げる,浴びせる,ひっかける throw away ~を捨てる;~を無駄に費やす,浪費する throw down 戦いを挑む
- **thrown** 動 throw(投げる)の過去分詞
- **thrust** 動 ①強く押す,押しつける,突き刺す ②張り出す,突き出る 名 ①ぐいと押すこと,突き刺すこと ②《the -》要点
- **tie** 動 結ぶ,束縛する
- **tiger** 名 トラ(虎)
- **time** 名 ①時,時間,歳月 ②時期 ③期間 ④時代 ⑤回,倍 at the time そのころ,当時は for the first time 初めて
- **tired** 形 ①疲れた,くたびれた ②あきた,うんざりした grow tired 飽きがくる
- **to** 前 ①《方向・変化》~へ,~に,~の方へ ②《程度・時間》~まで ③《適合・付加・所属》~に ④《- +動詞の原形》~するために[の],~する,~すること
- **together** 副 ①一緒に,ともに ②同時に
- **told** 動 tell(話す)の過去,過去分詞
- **tongue** 名 舌
- **tonight** 副 今夜は
- **too** 副 ①~も(また) ②あまりに~すぎる,とても~ That's too bad. 残念だ。 too much 過度の too ~

Short Stories of Ryunosuke Akutagawa

- to ……するには~すぎる
- **took** 動 take(取る)の過去
- **top** 名 頂上, 首位
- **Toribe Temple** 鳥部寺
- **torture** 動 拷問にかける, ひどく苦しめる
- **Toshishun** 名 杜子春《人名》
- **touch** 触れる, さわる, ~を触れさせる
- **toward** 前 ①《運動の方向・位置》~の方へ, ~に向かって ②《目的》~のために
- **town** 名 町, 都会, 都市
- **travel** 動 旅行する
- **treasure** 名 財宝, 貴重品, 宝物
- **tree** 名 木, 樹木
- **tried** 動 try(試みる)の過去, 過去分詞
- **trouble** 名 ①困難, 迷惑 ②心配, 苦労 ③もめごと
- **true** 形 ①本当の, 本物の, 真の ②誠実な, 確かな
- **truth** 名 ①真理, 事実, 本当 ②誠実, 忠実さ
- **try** 動 ①やってみる, 試みる ②努力する, 努める **try on** 試着してみる **try one's best** 全力を尽くす 名 試み, 試し
- **turn** 動 ①ひっくり返す, 回転する[させる], 曲がる, 曲げる, 向かう, 向ける ②(~に)なる, (~に)変える **turn out** ~と判明する **turn to** ~の方を向く, ~に頼る, ~に変わる
- **tweezers** 名 ピンセット, 毛抜き
- **twenty** 名 20(の数字), 20人[個] 形 20の, 20人[個]の
- **twenty-six** 形 26 の
- **twenty-third** 形 23 回目の
- **twice** 副 2倍, 2度, 2回
- **two** 名 2(の数字), 2人[個] 形 2の, 2人[個]の
- **type** 名 型, タイプ, 様式

U

- **under** 前 《位置》~の下[に]
- **understand** 動 理解する, わかる, ~を聞いて知っている
- **understood** 動 understand(理解する)の過去, 過去分詞
- **until** 前 ~まで(ずっと) 接 ~の時まで, ~するまで
- **up** 副 ①上へ, 上がって, 北へ ②立って, 近づいて ③向上して, 増して **be up to** ~の責任[義務]である **up to** ~まで, ~に至るまで, ~に匹敵して **up and down** 上がったり下がったり, 行ったり来たり, あちこちと 前 ①~の上(の方)へ, 高い方へ ②(道)に沿って
- **upper** 形 上の, 上位の, 北方の
- **us** 代 私たちを[に]
- **use** 動 ①使う, 用いる ②費やす 名 使用, 用途 **make use of** ~を利用する, ~を生かす
- **usually** 副 普通, いつも(は)

V

- **valley** 名 谷, 谷間
- **veil** 名 ベール, 覆い隠す物
- **very** 形 とても, 非常に, まったく **very well** 結構, よろしい
- **view** 動 眺める
- **visit** 動 訪問する
- **visitor** 名 訪問客
- **voice** 名 声, 音声

W

- **wait** 動 ①待つ, 《–for ~》~を待つ ②延ばす, 延ばせる, 遅らせる ③《–on [upon] ~》~に仕える, 給仕をする
- **Wakasa** 名 若狭《地名。現在の福井県西部》

Word List

- **walk** 動 歩く, 歩かせる, 散歩する walk along (前へ)歩く, 〜に沿って歩く walk away 立ち去る, 遠ざかる
- **walking** 形 徒歩の, 歩行用の
- **wall** 名 壁, 塀
- **want** 動 ほしい, 望む, 〜したい, 〜してほしい
- **warrior** 名 武人 demon warrior 神将
- **was** 動 《be の第1・第3人称単数現在 am, is の過去》〜であった, (〜に)いた[あった]
- **waste** 動 浪費する, 消耗する
- **watch** 動 じっと見る, 見物する
- **water** 名 水
- **way** 名 ①道, 通り道 ②方向, 距離 ③方法, 手段 ④習慣 all the way ずっと, はるばる, いろいろと along the way 途中で, これまでに, この先 give way 道を譲る, 譲歩する in a way ある意味では have one's way with 〜を思い通りにする look 〜 way 〜の方を見る make one's way through 〜の間を進む, 〜を通り抜ける on one's way 途中で one's way (to 〜) (〜への)途中で the same way as 〜と同様に this way このように way of 〜する方法 way to 〜する方法
- **we** 代 私たちは[が]
- **wear** 動 着る, 着ている, 身につける
- **week** 名 週, 1週間
- **well** 副 ①うまく, 上手に ②十分に, よく, かなり as well なお, その上, 同様に very well 結構, よろしい 間 へえ, まあ, ええと
- **went** 動 go (行く) の過去
- **were** 動 《be の2人称単数・複数の過去》〜であった, (〜に)いた[あった]
- **west** 名 《the –》西, 西部, 西方 形 西の, 西方[西部]の, 西向きの
- **what** 代 ①何が[を・に] ②《関係代名詞》〜するところのもの[こと] 形 ①何の, どんな ②なんと ③〜るだけの 副 いかに, どれほど
- **whatever** 代 ①《関係代名詞》〜するものは何でも ②どんなこと[もの]〜とも 形 ①どんな〜でも ②《否定文・疑問文で》少しの〜も, 何らかの
- **when** 副 ①いつ ②《関係代名詞》〜するところの, 〜するとその時, 〜するとき 接 〜の時, 〜するとき 代 いつ
- **where** 副 ①どこに[で] ②《関係副詞》〜するところの, そしてそこで, 〜するところ 接 〜なところに[へ], 〜するところに[へ] 代 ①どこ, どの点 ②〜するところの
- **whether** 接 〜かどうか, 〜かまたは…, 〜であろうとなかろうと whether or not 〜かどうか
- **which** 形 ①どちらの, どの, どれでも ②どちらの〜でも, どちらのこの 代 ①どちら, どれ, どの人[物] ②《関係代名詞》〜するところの
- **while** 接 ①〜の間(に), 〜する間(に) ②一方, 〜なのに 名 しばらくの間, 一定の時 after a while しばらくして for a while しばらくの間, 少しの間 once in a while たまに, 時々
- **whip** 名 むち
- **white** 形 白い
- **who** 代 ①誰が[は], どの人 ②《関係代名詞》〜するところの(人)
- **why** 副 ①なぜ, どうして ②《関係副詞》〜するところの(理由)
- **wife** 名 妻, 夫人
- **will** 助 〜だろう, 〜しよう, する(つもりだ)
- **wind** 名 風
- **window** 名 窓, 窓ガラス
- **wish** 動 望む, 願う, (〜であればよいと)思う
- **with** 前 ①《同伴・付随・所属》〜と一緒に, 〜を身につけて, 〜とともに ②《様態》〜で(の状態で), 〜して ③《手段・道具》〜で, 〜を使って with all 〜がありながら

Short Stories of Ryunosuke Akutagawa

- **without** 前 ～なしで，～がなく，～しないで
- **wizard** 名 (男の)魔法使い，仙人
- **woke** 動 wake (目が覚める)の過去
- **woman** 名 (成人した)女性，婦人
- **women** 名 woman (女性)の複数
- **won't** will not の短縮形
- **wonder** 動 ①不思議に思う，(～に)驚く ②(～かしらと)思う
- **wonderful** 形 驚くべき，すばらしい，すてきな
- **wood** 名 木材
- **woodcutter** 名 木こり
- **word** 名 ①語，単語 ②ひと言
- **wore** 動 wear (着ている)の過去
- **work** 動 ①働く，勉強する，取り組む ②機能[作用]する，うまくいく **work in** ～の分野で働く，～に入り込む **work of** ～の仕業 **work out** (問題を)解く，考え出す，答えが出る 名 ①仕事，勉強，職 ②作品
- **world** 名《the ‐》世界，～界
- **worry** 動 悩む，悩ませる，心配する[させる] **be worried about** (～のことで)心配している，～が気になる[かかる] **worry about** ～のことを心配する
- **worse** 形 いっそう悪い，より劣った，よりひどい 副 いっそう悪く
- **would** 助《will の過去》①～するだろう，～するつもりだ ②～したものだ **would like to** ～したいと思う
- **wound** 名 傷
- **wrong** 形 ①間違った，(道徳上)悪い ②調子が悪い，故障した 名 不正，悪事

Y・Z

- **Yamashina** 名 山科《地名。京都市》
- **year** 名 ①年，1年 ②学年，年度 ③～歳 **for ～ years** ～年間，～年にわたって
- **yes** 副 はい，そうです 名 肯定の言葉[返事]
- **yesterday** 名 ①昨日 ②過ぎし日，昨今 副 昨日(は)
- **yet** 副 ①《否定文で》まだ～(ない[しない]) ②《疑問文で》もう ③《肯定文で》まだ，今もなお 接 それにもかかわらず，しかし，けれども
- **you** 代 ①あなた(方)は[が]，あなた(方)を[に] ②(一般に)人は **you see** あのね，いいですか
- **young** 形 若い，幼い，青年の
- **your** 代 あなた(方)の
- **yours** 代 あなた(方)のもの
- **yourself** 代 あなた自身
- **Zenchi** 名 禅智《人名》

English Conversational Ability Test
国際英語会話能力検定

- **E-CATとは…**
英語が話せるようになるためのテストです。インターネットベースで、30分であなたの発話力をチェックします。

www.ecatexam.com

- **iTEP®とは…**
世界各国の企業、政府機関、アメリカの大学300校以上が、英語能力判定テストとして採用。オンラインによる90分のテストで文法、リーディング、リスニング、ライティング、スピーキングの5技能をスコア化。iTEP®は、留学、就職、海外赴任などに必要な、世界に通用する英語力を総合的に評価する画期的なテストです。

www.itepexamjapan.com

ラダーシリーズ
Short Stories of Ryunosuke Akutagawa
芥川龍之介短編集

2016年12月23日　第1刷発行
2024年7月11日　第4刷発行

原著者　芥川龍之介

発行者　賀川　洋

発行所　IBCパブリッシング株式会社
　　　　〒162-0804 東京都新宿区中里町29番3号
　　　　菱秀神楽坂ビル
　　　　Tel. 03-3513-4511　Fax. 03-3513-4512
　　　　www.ibcpub.co.jp

© Michael Brase 2016
© IBC Publishing. Inc. 2016

印刷　株式会社シナノパブリッシングプレス
装丁　伊藤 理恵　　カバー・本文イラスト　山田勇男
組版データ　Sabon Roman + ITC Tiepolo Std Bold

落丁本・乱丁本は、小社宛にお送りください。送料小社負担にてお取り替えいたします。
本書の無断複写（コピー）は著作権法上での例外を除き禁じられています。

Printed in Japan
ISBN 978-4-7946-0454-5